The Complete
PAINTED
FURNITURE
MANUAL

Jocasta Innes
& Stewart Walton

Paintability

conran
OCTOPUS

This edition first published in 1993 by Conran Octopus Limited
37 Shelton Street, London WC2H 9HN

Reprinted 1995, 1997

From an original idea by Stewart Walton and Jocasta Innes
Text and pattern copyright © Paintability 1991, 1992 and 1993

British Library Cataloguing-in-Publication Data
A catalogue record for this book is available from the British Library.

ISBN 1 85029 540 9

Printed in Hong Kong

Art Direction and Design : Robin Rout

Roomset Photography: James Merrell

Studio Photography: Tino Tedaldi

Set Building: Andy Knight

Set Painting: Steve Whittle

Styling (pages 8–79): Karina Garrick

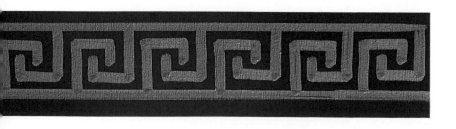

Contents

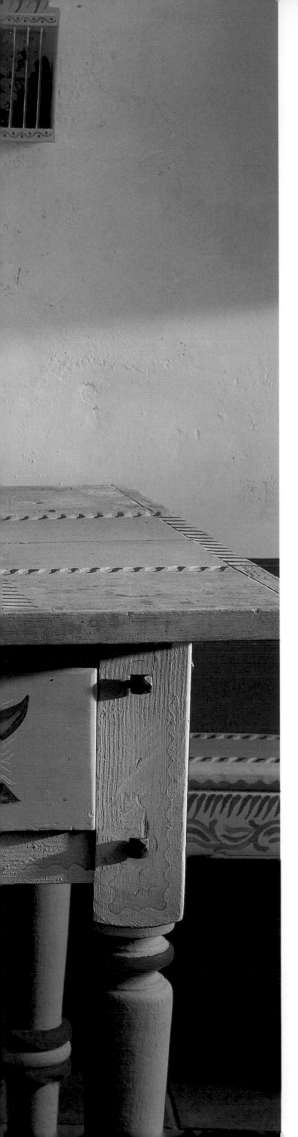

USING THE PATTERNS

At the end of each of the sections of this book you will find four pages of printed patterns that you can use to paint your furniture with a wide range of motifs to suit every style of interior: from hearts and flowers to folksy animals to classical lyres and wreaths. Start off by tracing the design or motif you want to use onto a sheet of good-quality tracing paper, available from art shops - it's particularly important you choose good-quality paper, especially for border and repeat motifs where you will be tracing over the outline a number of times. Some of the centrepiece designs contained in the book are shown across facing pages - simply trace off one side, then move the tracing paper across the page, match up the overlap and continue tracing to finish off the design.

Next, place a piece of standard carbon paper or chalked transfer paper, blue side down, in position on your chosen piece of furniture, and put the tracing paper on top of it. Carefully trace around the motif, pressing down firmly with a lead pencil - it will probably be much easier to trace around the design if you tape down the carbon paper and tracing paper in position first. Remove the masking tape and put the tracing and carbon paper to one side. The professionals' choice, chalked transfer paper is both quick and economical to use - by moving the paper around you can use the same piece again and again.

Now, using our suggested colour mixes and recommended paintbrushes, start to fill in the designs. It's as easy as painting by numbers - no design dilemmas, no chasing through source-books, no colour worries. The transferred outline is easy to see, yet can be wiped off with a damp cloth when the painted decoration is dry, removing any clues to your short-cut technique. The whole process is clearly explained and illustrated with easy-to-follow, step-by-step colour photographs and superb colour pictures of the finished results - from personalized painted furniture and accessories to a totally transformed room setting.

USING PAINTS

Where we've painted pieces of furniture in a base colour, we used standard matt emulsion paints, which are quick and easy to apply and which dry fast. They provide an excellent surface for decoration and, because they're water based, it's easy to clean your paintbrush after use - just give it a good soak in tap-water and scrub with an old scrubbing brush.

The motifs themselves are painted using either fast-drying artists' acrylic colours which are thinned down with a little water, or artists' gouache paints which are thinned down with a little gum arabic - all of these are readily available from craft shops and artists' suppliers. If you use gouache colours, you *must* remember to 'fix' it with a quick blast of spray varnish once the colour has dried but *before* you proceed to sealing it with a coat of varnish.

AUTHORS' TIP

There's no reason why you have to use the motifs the same size as we have in the book. If you want to squeeze a heart shape onto the top of a small trinket box or enlarge a starburst to fill a tabletop you can change the size to suit your needs. You don't need to go to the time and trouble of drawing up grids and copying the design laboriously - the simplest way by far is to use the reduction and enlargement facility on a photocopier. You can even photocopy directly onto a piece of tracing paper, making it quicker and easier than ever.

CHAPTER ONE

Simply FRENCH

The French really say it with flowers. Use our captivating posies, inspired by old regional pottery, to give rustic elegance to any country-style furniture. Add sprays, corner pieces and spot motifs.

Ring the changes with more florals and some chunkier borders. We think these stylised French designs look prettiest in simple colours like our blue-and-white pottery palette over spring-flower pastels.

PREPARE AND PAINT YOUR BACKGROUND

French country painting often shared the fresh colours of Breton rustic pottery. Primrose yellow, shades of French blue, and touches of white give the floral motifs a springlike charm.

Preparation can be minimal. Make sure surfaces are clean and non-greasy. Gloss finishes – paint or varnish – need sanding back with medium-grade sandpaper to provide a 'key' for the paint. No need to fill cracks and surface blemishes; these add character to a rustic painted piece. The kitchen cabinet and table shown here were both painted with standard matt emulsion paints. Emulsion is the modern decorator's choice because it dries fast, is easy to apply, and provides an excellent surface for decoration. In this case, it also imitates the 'lean' texture of eighteenth-century painted furniture, the result of using paints with a very low linseed oil content.

TO GIVE EXTRA DEPTH OF COLOUR TO PLAINLY PAINTED SURFACES, THE TECHNIQUE USED OVERLAYS TWO SHADES OF YELLOW MATT EMULSION, THE BRIGHTER COLOUR ON TOP. THE BRIGHT TOP COAT IS RUBBED BACK WITH MEDIUM-GRADE WET-AND-DRY PAPER JUST BEFORE IT DRIES. WET-AND-DRY PAPER, WHICH IS FINER THAN SANDPAPER, IS NOT ESSENTIAL, BUT AVOIDS THE RISK OF RUBBING THROUGH BOTH COATS.

TWO SHADES OF BLUE EMULSION HAVE BEEN USED HERE IN THE SAME WAY. NOTICE HOW THE STRONGER COLOUR EMPHASISES THE GUTSY TEXTURE AND GRAINING OF OLD WOODEN SURFACES.

A POSY OF COLOUR

The clear blues and yellows of our French-inspired kitchen corner are set off by a rich green background colour. Sophisticated rustic is the mood of traditional French painted decoration, and it is amazing what this artless style does for the unrelated assortment of pieces shown here – some of them antique, some plain junk – bringing them together harmoniously as part of an overall effect. Not all the pieces are wood. Toleware, or painted metal, is distinctively French and two examples are shown: a spoon rack and a delightful antique petrol can. On the rush-seated sofa motifs have been used sparingly, but these underline its attractive shape and character. The table is a very utilitarian kitchen piece with an enamelled top, transformed here with primrose paint and a blue flower spray. Note how carrying out a single colour theme 'ties' objects together.

PAINTING WITH A PATTERN

Painting simple little sprays will build up your confidence.

Shown here are the steps involved in tracing off and painting the simple pair of motifs we arranged to enhance the cut-out top of the wooden rail.

Points to remember: ● Use a hard lead pencil for the tracing down because this will give you a clear outline. ● Keep a clean copy of the tracing patterns – you might like to photocopy them a few times. You can then cut them up to fit awkward spaces without worrying about losing the originals. ● If you cut smaller pieces of transfer paper, be careful to leave yourself a big enough piece for the largest motif. ● Most of the patterns in this book were painted with fast-drying artist's acrylic colours, available in tubes from all artist's suppliers. These dry with a matt finish, and are used thinned with a little water to 'single cream' consistency. Use an old plate as a palette. ● Use soft watercolour brushes in different sizes to paint motifs, including one fine one for outlining. There is no need to buy expensive sable brushes – synthetic bristles or mixed hair are fine.

TRACING DOWN AND FILLING IN

Symmetrical patterns are easy to do and always look at home in this style of rustic decoration.

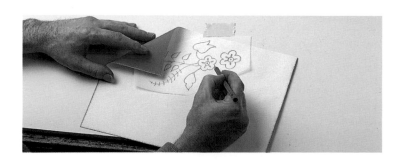

1 FIX PATTERN IN PLACE WITH MASKING TAPE. SLIP TRANSFER PAPER BENEATH. TRACE PATTERNS CAREFULLY AND FIRMLY WITH SHARP PENCIL.

2 USE CENTRAL FLOWER TO LINE UP SECOND HALF OF SYMMETRICAL FLOWER SPRAY. (TURN TRACING OVER.)

3 USING MEDIUM BRUSH, FILL IN PATTERN SHAPES (EXCEPT STEMS) WITH COLOUR A.

4 WITH FINER BRUSH, USE COLOUR B TO PAINT IN OUTLINES. USE VERY LIGHT PRESSURE WHEN PAINTING FINE STEMS OR LEAFY TENDRILS.

MATERIALS CHECKLIST

WELL-SHARPENED HARD LEAD PENCIL, SCISSORS, MASKING TAPE, OLD PLATE, WATER JAR, KITCHEN PAPER OR TISSUES FOR WIPING BRUSHES, RULER OR TAPE FOR POSITIONING MOTIFS.

ACRYLIC COLOURS IN WHITE, RAW UMBER, COBALT AND ULTRAMARINE BLUE.

TWO WATERCOLOUR BRUSHES, ONE FINE, ONE MEDIUM.

COLOUR RECIPES:
(A) WHITE WITH TOUCH OF RAW UMBER
(B) ULTRAMARINE WITH TOUCH OF RAW UMBER

5 BALANCED ARRANGEMENTS ARE USED ON COUNTRY FURNITURE FOR HIGHLIGHTING DECORATIVE SHAPES: CHAIRBACKS, BEDHEADS, THE CORNICE OF A DRESSER OR CUPBOARD, FOR EXAMPLE. THERE IS AN ALMOST CALLIGRAPHIC QUALITY TO THESE STROKES. PRACTICE WILL ENABLE YOU TO ACHIEVE THE SAME EFFECT, AND TO EXECUTE EACH STROKE IN ONE SWEEP OF THE BRUSH.

PAINTERLY TRICKS OF THE TRADE

The decoration on small objects that are handled and looked at closely needs to be more controlled and subtle. Here we show some ideas for you to copy in order to add quality to your painting.

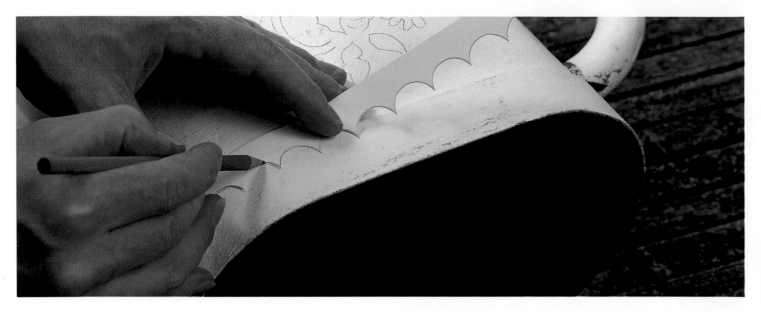

1 THERE IS NO NEED TO KEEP REPEATING THE SAME SIMPLE BORDER TRACING. CUTTING A CARD TEMPLATE LIKE THE ONE HERE, AND USING IT TO PENCIL AROUND AN OBJECT, MAKES THE JOB MUCH QUICKER. INDIVIDUAL BRUSH STROKES WILL GIVE THIS DESIGN MUCH MORE VIVACITY THAN IF IT WERE CAREFULLY AND EVENLY FILLED IN.

3 FORM 'LEAF' SHAPES NATURALLY AND EASILY WITH A SOFT WATERCOLOUR BRUSH. APPLY BRUSH TO SURFACE, PRESS AND GENTLY RELEASE OUT OF STROKE. 'COMMA' SHAPES FOR PETALS ARE FORMED BY APPLYING GREATER PRESSURE INITIALLY BEFORE TAPERING OUT.

4 THE 'DRY BRUSH' TECHNIQUE IS USED TO GIVE TEXTURE AND FORM TO ROSE PETALS. BLOT MOST OF COLOUR OFF ON KITCHEN PAPER, AND TEST BRUSH ON SHEET OF PAPER FIRST. THERE SHOULD BE JUST ENOUGH COLOUR ON THE BRUSH TO LEAVE A CLOUDY LINE.

AUTHORS' TIP It really is worth practising making brush strokes like the ones shown here on spare sheets of paper before launching on a piece as attractive as this. The whole expressiveness of this type of decoration lies in the spontaneity and variety of the brush strokes.

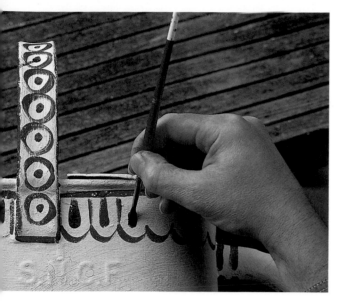

2 MAKE YOUR BRUSH WORK FOR YOU. THE CHARM OF THIS VERY BASIC BORDER MOTIF COMES FROM THE LOOSE AND IMPRESSIONISTIC USE OF BRUSH STROKES TO 'DASH' IN THE SHAPES.

5 THE COMPLETED PETROL CAN SHOWS THIS SORT OF DECORATIVE PAINTING AT ITS SPIRITED BEST: PRACTICE IS NEEDED TO PERFECT LOOSENESS IN BRUSH TECHNIQUE.

COLOUR RECIPE

ONE COLOUR USED FOR ALL STAGES:
ULTRAMARINE BLUE WITH TOUCH OF RAW UMBER

ACRYLIC MEDIUM, ALSO CALLED PVA, CAN BE MIXED WITH ANY ACRYLIC COLOUR FOR THINNER PAINT AND HENCE GREATER FLOW.

1 USING COLOUR A, BRUSH IN ALL MAIN
OUTLINES, STEMS AND LEAVES.

4 COLOUR C IS USED TO HIGHLIGHT LEAF SHAPES
AND TO ADD DOTS.

COLOUR RECIPES

(A) ULTRAMARINE WITH TOUCH OF RAW UMBER

(B) 2 PARTS COBALT BLUE, ONE PART WHITE,
TOUCH OF RAW UMBER

(C) WHITE WITH TOUCH OF ULTRAMARINE BLUE

By now you are beginning to feel relaxed and confident with your brushwork. A different approach is being used here for the main flower piece in our French painting patterns. All the main outlines are brushed in first with blue, as expressively possible.

2 FILL IN PETALS AND SOME LEAF SHAPES USING COLOUR B TOWARDS OUTSIDE AND COLOUR C TOWARDS MIDDLE.

3 PAIRS OF LEAVES ARE DRAWN OFF CENTRAL STEM IN COLOUR A. HERE, BRUSH STROKES BEGIN FINE, THEN ROUND OUT TO CREATE LEAVES.

5 SMALL PENDANT DESIGN IS BRUSHED IN DOWN TABLE LEG USING COLOUR A.

6 THESE SHAPES ARE HIGHLIGHTED AND SOFTENED WITH COLOUR B.

AUTHOR'S TIPS
The painting hand often needs support when working in the middle of a surface. Usually, resting it on your free hand provides a steadying base. As it is invariably easier to paint designs on a horizontal surface, on tricky shapes try turning the piece, and tip furniture on its side as necessary. Also, most painting of this sort has a 'direction', so always orient yourself appropriately.

FITTING
FLOWERS

*Play around with your pattern elements before
deciding which looks best where.*

Flower sprays and borders are ideal for long narrow spaces,
like the side of this table, or the little drop ornament on the
leg. The narrow formal border makes a feature of the
attractive shape of the rush-seated sofa. You need to spend
more time on the planning than on the actual painting in
many cases.

THE LARGE FLORAL MOTIF, CARRIED OUT IN FULL COLOUR ON THE
ENAMEL TABLE TOP, ALMOST HAS THE LOOK OF HAND-PAINTED
PORCELAIN. THE PAINTS USED ARE TRANSPARENT GLASS PAINTS,
OBTAINABLE FROM SPECIALIST TRADE SHOPS. THESE PAINTS ARE
ALMOST AS HARD AS ENAMEL SO ON A SURFACE LIKE THIS A
VARNISH IS NOT NECESSARY. THE PAINTABILITY TRANSFER PAPER
DOES NOT GIVE CLEAR IMPRESSIONS ON A SHINY SURFACE LIKE
THIS: HERE WE SUBSTITUTED ORDINARY CARBON PAPER.

THE SAME MOTIF INTERPRETED IN THE SAME COLOURS, YET ON A DIFFERENT BACKGROUND COLOUR AND ARRANGED DIFFERENTLY, CAN PRODUCE A SURPRISINGLY DISTINCTIVE RESULT. THE 'PAIR OF LEAVES' BORDER IS USED ON THE FRAME OF THE SOFA AND THE SIDE OF THE TABLE. ON THE SOFA, CURVING IT SLIGHTLY AND TAPERING IT OFF TOWARDS THE BOTTOM GIVES IT A MUCH MORE DELICATE EFFECT.

It takes very little time to decorate small items like the quartet on this page, but the results can be charming.

CLEVER RE-JUGGLING OF THE BASIC PATTERN MOTIFS HAS MADE A DELIGHTFUL OBJECT OF AN ANTIQUE FRENCH PETROL CAN. THE BORDERS EMPHASISE THE SHAPE OF THE CAN VERY ATTRACTIVELY. NOTE THE LIVELY BRUSH STROKES WHICH GIVE THE FLOWER SPRAY SO MUCH CHARACTER. ACRYLIC PAINTS OVER AN EMULSION BASE WERE USED HERE.

THIS LITTLE CABINET WITH ITS BEVELLED PORTHOLE MIRROR IS AN IDEAL PIECE TO PAINT, SO DECORATIVE IN ITSELF THAT IT ONLY NEEDED A LITTLE HELP FROM OUR PAINTING PATTERNS.

THE SAME FLOWER SPRAY AS ON THE SPOON RACK, SLIGHTLY ADJUSTED, IS PAINTED WITH ACRYLIC COLOURS ON A FLAT EMULSION BASE. THIS IS ACTUALLY AN AUTHENTIC FRENCH MAILBOX, LOOKING PRETTY ENOUGH TO BE PROMOTED TO THE KITCHEN.

THE UTILITARIAN CHARACTER OF AN ENAMEL SPOON RACK HAS
BEEN COMPLETELY DISGUISED BY THE FRENCH FLOWER SPRAY,
CARRIED OUT IN TWO SHADES OF BLUE ONLY. USING GLASS
PAINTS AGAIN HAS GIVEN A WATERCOLOUR-LIKE TRANSPARENCY
TO THE STANDARD MOTIF.

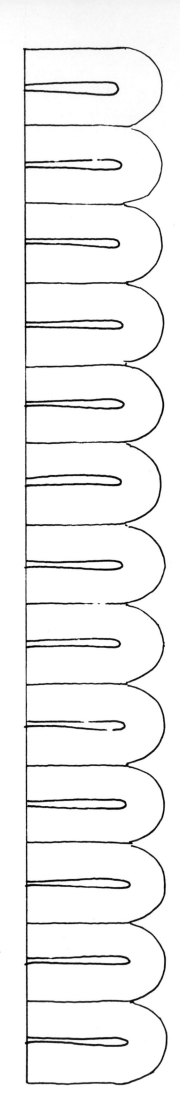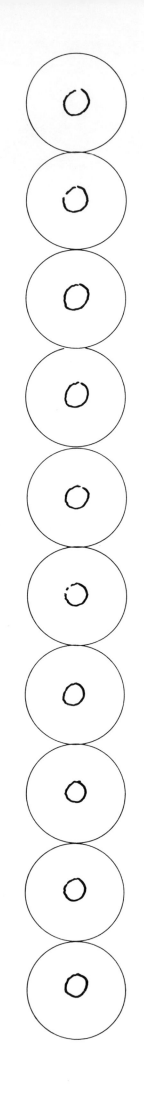

CHAPTER TWO

Simply SCANDINAVIAN

Scandinavian furniture painters often produced breathtaking effects using the simplest motifs. Single brush strokes combine to create a flowing border and spot motifs in rococo style. For contrast, spiky geometrics and that eternal favourite, the heart symbol of love, complete the collection.

Derived from seventeenth-century flower paintings, the handsome floral arrangements are an enduringly popular feature of all folk painting. Great for panel filling, for centring on a bedhead, or for dramatising a dull kitchen unit.

PREPARE AND PAINT YOUR BACKGROUND

Scandinavian painted furniture draws on the rich, deep colours popular in that part of Europe during the Baroque period of the late seventeenth century.

Preparation can be minimal. Make sure surfaces are clean and non-greasy. Gloss finishes – paint or varnish – need sanding back with medium-grade sandpaper to provide a 'key' for the paint. No need to fill cracks and surface blemishes; these add character to a rustic painted piece. The sturdy stool and pine cabinet were both painted using standard matt emulsion paints, intermixed for colour variations. Emulsion is the modern decorator's choice because it drys fast, is easy to apply, and provides an excellent surface for decoration. In this case, it also imitates the 'dry' texture of traditional home-made paints based on ingredients like buttermilk, egg yolk, fruit juice or berries, and seaweed.

TO GIVE EXTRA DEPTH OF COLOUR THE RED SURFACES OF THE STOOL WERE PAINTED WITH RUSTY RED MATT EMULSION OVER A WARM CREAM EMULSION. WHEN DRY THE TOP COAT WAS RUBBED BACK WITH MEDIUM-GRADE SANDPAPER – OR DAMPENED WET-AND-DRY PAPER – TO GIVE GLIMPSES OF THE PALER COLOUR BENEATH. THE BLUE SURFACES HAVE BEEN VERY LIGHTLY DISTRESSED IN THE SAME WAY.

DEEP EARTHY SHADES LIKE THE ONES USED HERE TRANSFORM A SIMPLE RUSTIC LAUNDRY BASKET INTO SOMETHING QUITE SPECIAL. BOLDNESS BOTH IN COLOUR AND IN DESIGN IS EVERYTHING WITH THE FOLK STYLE OF PAINTED FURNITURE DECORATION. EXPERIMENT WITH DIFFERENT COLOUR VARIATIONS UNTIL YOU FIND ONE THAT SUITS YOUR DECOR.

THE HEARTY COLOURS OF

Scandinavian rural painters used colour to counteract the tedium of winter darkness, so that the interiors of wooden cabins were often as vivid as flower gardens. Softwood furniture was invariably painted to add colour and excitement against a background of dusky wooden plank and log walls. A warm, blood red is still a favourite colour in Nordic countries, used for clothes and embroideries, as well as in furniture decoration. It is

OLD SCANDINAVIA

usually balanced with the deep blue-green used here as the base colour on the sturdy, homely pieces of furniture in this Scandinavian-style cottage. Look for chunky items of furniture to paint with the Scandinavian patterns.

Panels like the ones on the settle and the small cupboard are ideal for folk motifs. Keeping to the same base colour throughout is a good way of linking together disparate items from different periods.

PAINTING WITH A PATTERN

Start with simple motifs in a few colours – none of the patterns used here is difficult to paint.

Shown here are the steps involved in tracing off and painting the daisy border and yellow heart motif which give so much character to the simple wooden stool.

Points to remember: ● Use a hard lead pencil for the tracing down because this will give you a clear outline. ● Keep a clean copy of the tracing patterns – you might like to photocopy them a few times. You can then cut them up to fit awkward spaces without worrying about losing the originals. ● If you cut smaller pieces of transfer paper, be careful to leave yourself a big enough piece for the largest

TRACING DOWN AND FILLING IN

Repeating patterns are easy to apply and always look convincing in this style of rustic decoration.

1 FIX PATTERN IN PLACE WITH MASKING TAPE. SLIP TRANSFER PAPER BENEATH.

2 WITH SHARP PENCIL TRACE OFF MAIN OUTLINES OF DAISY PATTERN.

3 USING MEDIUM BRUSH AND COLOUR A, DAB IN DAISY PETALS, ONE STROKE TO EACH PETAL, WITHOUT TRYING TO MAKE THEM TOO REGULAR.

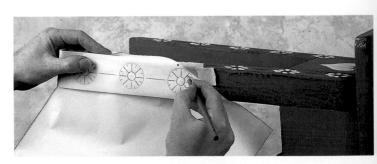

4 BOLD RED (COLOUR B) AND FINER BRUSH ARE USED TO PAINT LINKING LEAF SHAPES AND DAISY CENTRES.

motif. ● All the patterns in this book were painted with fast-drying artist's acrylic colours, available in tubes from all artist's suppliers. These dry with a matt finish, and are used thinned with a little water to 'single cream' consistency. Use an old plate as a palette. ● Use soft watercolour brushes in different sizes to paint motifs, including one fine one for outlining. There is no need to buy expensive sable brushes – synthetic bristles or mixed hair are fine.

MATERIALS CHECKLIST

WELL-SHARPENED HARD LEAD PENCIL, SCISSORS, MASKING TAPE, OLD PLATE, WATER JAR, KITCHEN PAPER OR TISSUES FOR WIPING BRUSHES, RULER OR TAPE FOR POSITIONING MOTIFS.

ACRYLIC COLOURS IN ULTRAMARINE BLUE, COBALT, RAW UMBER, WHITE, CADMIUM RED AND CHROME YELLOW.

THREE WATERCOLOUR BRUSHES, ONE FINE, ONE MEDIUM, ONE LARGE.

COLOUR RECIPES: (A) WHITE WITH TOUCH OF RAW UMBER

(B) CADMIUM RED WITH TOUCH OF RAW UMBER

(C) COLOUR A WITH TOUCH OF CHROME YELLOW

5 WHEN PAINTING A LIGHTER COLOUR SUCH AS THE YELLOW (COLOUR C) OVER A DARK COLOUR LIKE THIS RED, IT IS A GOOD IDEA TO PAINT IN THE MOTIF FIRST WITH A LIGHT OR WHITE UNDERCOAT. THIS WILL MAKE YOUR COLOURS FRESH AND GLOWING.

EXUBERANT CLASSICAL MOTIFS ARE

Many traditional motifs from the Rococo period were built up with swirling, curving brush strokes. Practise these on spare paper until they flow confidently.

1 SECTION OF ROCOCO BORDER TAPED TO THE SURFACE, PRIOR TO TRACING OFF. RATHER THAN DRAW AROUND EACH LEAF, SIMPLY DRAW IN CENTRAL 'VEIN'. THIS SAVES TIME AND CREATES SPONTANEITY.

2 USE COLOUR A AND LARGE BRUSH TO FILL IN ELONGATED TEARDROP SHAPES. NOTE TRACING IS MINIMAL ON LEAVES AND BRUSH IS BEING USED TO BLOCK IN SHAPES.

1 USE MEDIUM BRUSH, WELL LOADED WITH COLOUR C, TO MAKE REGULAR DOTS AND FLOWER SHAPES. A GENTLE PRESSURE IS ALL THAT IS NEEDED. COLOUR D FORMS CENTRE.

COLOUR RECIPES

(A) 2 PARTS ULTRAMARINE BLUE, 2 PARTS WHITE, 1 PART COBALT, 1 PART RAW UMBER

(B) ULTRAMARINE BLUE WITH TOUCH OF RAW UMBER

(C) WHITE WITH TOUCH OF RAW UMBER

(D) CADMIUM RED WITH TOUCH OF RAW UMBER

GIVEN THE FOLK TREATMENT

3 USE CLEAN LARGE BRUSH AND COLOUR B TO ADD DARKER 'TADPOLE' SHAPES.

4 USE MEDIUM BRUSH AND COLOUR C TO 'DRY BRUSH' HIGHLIGHTS OVER PALE BLUE SHAPES. PICK UP COLOUR ON BRUSH, THEN RUB MOST OF IT OFF ON KITCHEN PAPER BEFORE STARTING. TEST BRUSH ON SHEET OF PAPER FIRST. THERE SHOULD BE JUST ENOUGH COLOUR TO LEAVE A CLOUDY LINE.

1 FAT SCROLL SHAPES, ADDED TOGETHER, CREATE A CHARACTERISTIC MOTIF IN SCANDINAVIAN PAINTED DECORATION. NOTE HOW SCROLL SHAPES ARE SIMPLY TRACED OFF AS LINES.

2 'DRY BRUSH' TECHNIQUE IS USED TO DRAMATISE THE MOTIF BLOCKED IN WITH COLOUR A. COLOUR B CREATES A SHADOW. 'DRY BRUSHING' WITH C DRAGS ON HIGHLIGHTS.

AUTHORS' TIP
Supporting your brush hand with your other hand helps to steady your brush. This makes all the difference in achieving steady, controlled brush strokes, especially in the middle of a large painted area.

1 BRUSH IN ALL TRACE-DOWN SHAPES WITH COLOUR A AND MEDIUM BRUSH. THESE INCLUDE LEAVES, 'TADPOLES' AND DOTS.

4 USE COLOUR C AND LARGE BRUSH TO 'WHISK' IN PLUM 'TADPOLE' SHAPES ON VASE AND CENTRAL LEAF SHAPE

COLOUR RECIPES

(A) 2 PARTS ULTRAMARINE BLUE, 2 PARTS WHITE, 1 PART COBALT, 1 PART RAW UMBER

(B) ULTRAMARINE BLUE WITH TOUCH OF RAW UMBER

(C) WHITE WITH TOUCH OF RAW UMBER

By now you are beginning to feel relaxed and confident with your brushwork. A different approach is being used here for the floral set piece in our Scandinavian painting pattern. The same three shades of dark blue, light blue and off white are used to create a vigorous panel-filler, showing stylised flowers and leaves in a classical-type urn.

2 COLOUR B IS USED WITH A CLEAN MEDIUM BRUSH TO FATTEN UP THE DESIGN AS SHOWN AND SUGGEST STRONG SHADING AROUND MAIN SHAPES.

3 COLOUR C AND A FINE BRUSH PICK OUT DETAILS, HIGHLIGHTS AND FLOURISHES THAT ADD GREATLY TO THE CHARM OF SCANDINAVIAN DESIGN.

5 THE CLOSE-UP SHOWS HOW EFFECTIVE SMALL 'FLICKS' OF WHITE (COLOUR C) ARE IN ADDING LIVELINESS AND RICHNESS TO A FOLK DESIGN.

6 TO FILL A LONG ELONGATED SPACE, THE WHOLE BOUQUET MOTIF CAN BE REVERSED AND TRACED OFF JUST BELOW THE FIRST, CREATING THE EFFECTS SHOWN.

AUTHORS' TIPS
Norwegian 'Rosmaling' painters stress that it is much harder to paint the left-hand side of a symmetrical shape. If this is your problem, try turning the piece around.

A STARRY INTERIOR

Play around with your pattern elements before deciding which looks best where.

A rich mix of motifs on the same piece gives this stocky little cabinet a peculiarly Scandinavian charm. Many old Norwegian cupboards were decorated inside as a background to the family's prized pewter, china or linen.

THE ARTLESS DAISY DRESSES UP THE SIMPLEST WOODEN COAT OR CUP RACK. THE SAME DAISY MOTIF MAKES AN APPEALING DECORATION AROUND THE TOP OF A QUAINTLY RUSTIC TABLE WITH A BASE MADE OF JOINED-UP TWIGS. THE SCROLL SHAPES MAKE A HIGHLY DECORATIVE FRAME FOR THE DATE PAINTED IN THE MIDDLE OF THE TABLE. FOLK PAINTERS LOVED ADDING PERSONAL TOUCHES LIKE THESE. A SET OF INITIALS WAS ANOTHER COMMON CHOICE.

FOLK PATTERNS AS BRIGHT AS THESE INVARIABLY LOOK BEST ON A DISTRESSED BACKGROUND COLOUR. HERE THE DARK BLUE-GREEN EMULSION PAINT HAS BEEN RUBBED BACK FIERCELY ON THE OUTER EDGES OF DRAWERS AND DOORS TO REVEAL THE WOOD. TO SOFTEN THE BASE COLOUR FURTHER THE WHOLE PIECE WAS THEN WASHED OVER WITH ULTRAMARINE BLUE HEAVILY DILUTED WITH WATER, THEN RUBBED OFF WITH A RAG HERE AND THERE. THIS GIVES A CERTAIN DEPTH TO THE COLOUR.

JOIN THE TWO PATTERN HALVES TO MAKE UP THE MOTIF

CHAPTER THREE

Simply MEXICAN

Brilliant as cactus flowers, Mexican painted decoration traditionally draws on the richness of peasant embroidery together with dazzling colour contrasts. You can really let yourself go, adding vibrant colour and exuberant brush strokes to transform drab pieces of furniture. Simple but punchy borders build up layer upon layer of chunky designs for a dramatic framed effect.

Paint your own Mexican Pueblo street with our delightful house-front patterns. Ideal for adding naive charm to chests, tin trunks and hat boxes. The floral designs can be used as a main centrepiece or repeated as an edging. Tiny borders add the finishing touch.

PREPARE AND PAINT YOUR BACKGROUND

Mexican colours are vivid, going on for gaudy. Matt textures and chalky hues create the look.

Preparation can be minimal. Make sure surfaces are clean and non-greasy. Gloss finishes – paint or varnish – need sanding back with medium-grade sandpaper to provide a 'key' for the paint. No need to fill cracks and surface blemishes; these add character to a rustic painted piece. The pieces shown here were all painted with standard matt emulsion paints, intermixed for colour variation. Emulsion is the modern decorator's choice because it drys fast, is easy to apply, and provides an excellent surface for decoration. See below for ways of creating unusual effects with these standard paints, like the two-tone shades which imitate the patina of antique colour.

A CHARACTERISTICALLY MEXICAN EFFECT COMES FROM COMBINING STRONGLY SATURATED AND CONTRASTING COLOURS, AS SEEN HERE IN OUR ATTRACTIVE LATTICE WALL CUPBOARD, WHICH HAS BEEN PAINTED SHARP GREEN OUTSIDE AND BRIGHT PINK INSIDE.

THE RICH GLOW OF THE LIME GREEN FINISH ON OUR MEXICAN BENCH COMES FROM APPLYING A COAT OF SAP GREEN EMULSION ON TOP OF A CANARY YELLOW EMULSION. WHEN DRY THE GREEN COAT IS RUBBED DOWN CAREFULLY WITH DAMPENED MEDIUM-GRADE WET-AND-DRY PAPER, UNTIL THE YELLOW LAYER BEGINS TO SHOW THROUGH.

COLOURFUL AS A MEXICAN

South of the border, colour becomes as exciting as a firework display. Traditional Mexican embroideries with brilliant florals inspired many of the painted patterns shown in this vivid corner of a patio. What

traditional Mexican folk art teaches us is that the right clash of contrasting colours is wonderfully stimulating. Colours used here range from sharp pastels – lime green, cactus-flower pink, ochre yellow – to deep feisty

PONCHO

blues and reds, popular with peasant painters the world over. Patterns in this set include a stunning flower piece, shown here around a standard kitchen table, a charming pueblo street scene used to decorate a wooden blanket box, plus a clutch of lively border designs. As the results prove, the Mexican message where colours are concerned is not to be afraid of mixing it.

PAINTING WITH A PATTERN

Start with an undemanding border pattern to give yourself confidence and test out your tracing and brushwork.

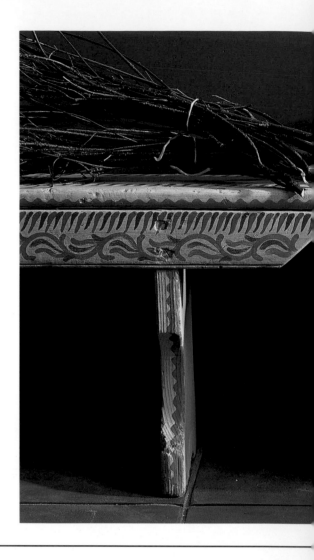

Shown here are the steps involved in tracing off and painting the simple border motifs we arranged to enhance the side of a long wooden bench.

Points to remember: ● Use a hard lead pencil for the tracing down because this will give you a clear outline. ● Keep a clean copy of the tracing patterns – you might like to photocopy them a few times. You can then cut them up to fit awkward spaces without worrying about losing the originals. ● If you cut smaller pieces of transfer paper, be careful to leave yourself a big enough piece for the largest motif. ● Most of the patterns in this book were painted with fast-drying artist's acrylic colours, available in tubes from all artist's suppliers.

TRACING DOWN AND FILLING IN

You may find it easier to cut individual motifs from your pattern sheet, and cut smaller pieces of transfer paper.

1 FIX PATTERN IN PLACE WITH MASKING TAPE. SLIP TRANSFER PAPER BENEATH.

2 TRACE PATTERNS CAREFULLY AND FIRMLY WITH SHARP PENCIL.

5 ALTERNATE 'TADPOLE' SHAPES ARE BRUSHED IN WITH FINE BRUSH AND COLOUR A. START BRUSH STROKES AT THE TAPERING END, GRADUALLY INCREASING PRESSURE.

6 COLOUR A AND FINE BRUSH ARE USED AGAIN TO CREATE SWEEPING CURVES OF SECOND BORDER DESIGN. PAINT LARGER CURVES FIRST THEN ADD SMALLER LEAF SHAPES.

These dry with a matt finish, and are used thinned with a little water to 'single cream' consistency. Use an old plate as a palette. ● Use soft watercolour brushes in different sizes to paint motifs, including one fine one for outlining. There is no need to buy expensive sable brushes – synthetic bristles or mixed hair are fine.

MATERIALS CHECKLIST

WELL-SHARPENED HARD LEAD PENCIL, SCISSORS, MASKING TAPE, OLD PLATE, WATER JAR, KITCHEN PAPER OR TISSUES FOR WIPING BRUSHES, RULER OR TAPE FOR POSITIONING MOTIFS.

ACRYLIC COLOURS IN WHITE, ULTRAMARINE BLUE, CADMIUM RED, YELLOW OCHRE AND HOOKER'S GREEN.

TWO WATERCOLOUR BRUSHES, ONE FINE, ONE MEDIUM.

COLOUR RECIPES:

(A) ULTRAMARINE BLUE WITH TOUCH OF WHITE

(B) CADMIUM RED WITH TOUCH OF YELLOW OCHRE

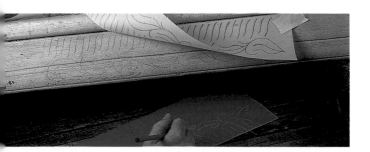

3 TRACED DOWN PATTERNS APPEAR CLEARLY ON PAINTED SURFACE.

4 WITH A SIMPLE WAVE DESIGN LIKE THIS YOU CAN DRAW AROUND A TEMPLATE FOR SPEED. MAKE YOUR OWN TEMPLATE BY TRACING OFF THE 'WAVE' BORDER ONTO CARD.

7 COLOUR A AND MEDIUM BRUSH ARE USED TO COLOUR IN 'WAVE' DESIGN, OUTLINED WITH TEMPLATE. USE FREE HAND TO STEADY PAINTING HAND AND BRUSH.

8 A CLEAN FINE BRUSH AND COLOUR B ARE USED TO BRING THE WHOLE BORDER TO LIFE WITH FLASHES OF CHILLI RED.

1 USE FREE HAND TO STEADY PAINTING HAND AS YOU BRUSH IN WHITE 'EYE' SHAPES WITH COLOUR A. DON'T WORRY ABOUT LOOSENESS IN EXECUTION.

2 SIZE OF BRUSH DETERMINES THICKNESS OF STROKE. A FINER BRUSH IS USED TO ADD SLENDER LEAF SHAPES.

2 DOUBLING UP ONE MOTIF CREATES A TWO-STOREY COLONNADED BUILDING. REMEMBER A SHARP PENCIL HELPS GREATLY IN TRACING OFF MOTIFS CLEARLY.

3 USING COLOURS C, D AND E AND MEDIUM BRUSH, COLOUR IN BASIC FOLIAGE AND BUILDING SHAPES.

COLOUR RECIPES

(A) WHITE WITH TOUCH OF CADMIUM RED
(B) CADMIUM RED
(C) WHITE
(D) YELLOW OCHRE WITH A LITTLE WHITE
(E) HOOKER'S GREEN WITH TOUCH OF WHITE AND YELLOW OCHRE
(F) 2 PARTS CADMIUM RED, 1 PART YELLOW OCHRE
(G) HOOKER'S GREEN

BORDERLINE BRILLIANCE

Simple borders made up of two or three colours are fun to do and look excitingly rich in these two Mexican designs.

3 COLOUR B IS USED TO DASH IN SQUIGGLES AND CROSS-HATCHING.

1 BUILDING BLOCK SYSTEM IS USED TO CREATE PUEBLO STREET SCENE FROM A FEW BASIC ELEMENTS. USE IDEAS HERE AS INSPIRATION.

4 USE SINGLE BRUSH STROKE TO MAKE TREE TRUNKS. SWITCH TO FINE BRUSH AND COLOUR F TO ADD FINER BUILDING DETAILS.

5 IMPROVISED DETAILING AS SHOWN HERE CAN ADD IMPACT TO YOUR PAINTED DESIGNS. THERE IS NO NEED TO BE TOO ELABORATE. TREE SHAPES ARE SIMPLY SHADED WITH COLOUR G.

AUTHORS' TIP
Don't be afraid to improvise by adding to, or juggling with, basic patterns. Practise alternatives first on paper so you don't lose spontaneity.

1 TRACED DOWN PAPER PATTERN FOR THE MEXICAN FLOWER PIECE SHOWING THE BLUE LINE TO FOLLOW FOR PAINTING ON THE GREEN TABLE. NOTE: THE MAIN ROSE MOTIF DETAILS ARE PAINTED OVER THE FIRST COLOUR LAYER. EITHER RE-TRACE THE DETAILS OR USE THE TRACING AS A GUIDE TO PAINT THEM FREEHAND.

4 COLOUR C IS USED TO FILL IN SMALL FLOWER SHAPES WHICH ARE THEN HIGHLIGHTED WITH COLOUR D.

5 WHITE HIGHLIGHTS (COLOUR D) ADD TYPICAL FOLKSY CONTRAST. USE A FINE BRUSH AND PRACTISE A LITTLE ON PAPER FIRST TO ACHIEVE FLUENT BUT DELICATE STROKES.

AUTHORS' TIPS
As it is invariably easier to paint designs on a horizontal surface, on tricky shapes try turning the piece, and tip furniture on its side as necessary. Also, most painting of this sort has a 'direction', so always orient yourself appropriately.

Having cut your teeth on the simpler patterns, it is time to have fun with colour and the exuberant floral motifs which make such a stunning addition to your painted furniture.

2 COLOUR A IS USED TO FILL IN THE RED ROSE AND PAIR OF BUDS. USE A MEDIUM BRUSH.

3 USING COLOUR B FILL IN GREEN LEAF SHAPES AND CALYXES.

6 FINISHING TOUCHES: A YELLOW CENTRE (COLOUR E) AND DARKER SHADING (COLOUR F) MAKE THE ROSE MORE VIVID STILL, PLUS LIGHTER GREEN (COLOUR G) HIGHLIGHTS LEAVES.

7 THIS DETAIL SHOWS HOW THE FLORAL DESIGN CAN EASILY BE EXPANDED. TO EXTEND ON THE OTHER SIDE, FLIP THE TRACING OVER.

COLOUR RECIPES

(A) CADMIUM RED

(B) HOOKER'S GREEN

(C) WHITE WITH TOUCH OF ULTRAMARINE BLUE

(D) WHITE

(E) YELLOW OCHRE

(F) CADMIUM RED WITH TOUCH OF ULTRAMARINE BLUE

(G) HOOKER'S GREEN WITH TOUCH OF YELLOW OCHRE AND WHITE

PUNCHY DETAILS RAISE THE COLOUR TEMPERATURE

Hot sunny colours sing out against a deep blue background colour. Simple shapes are completely transformed by our Mexican designs.

A POSSE OF PATTERN. IT DOES NOT NEED A LOT OF PAINT TO TRANSFORM SMALLER ITEMS LIKE THE PRETTY DECORATIVE CAGES AND BOTTLE BASKET SHOWN HERE. NOTE HOW DIFFERENT THE 'TADPOLE' BORDER LOOKS EXECUTED IN DIFFERENT COLOURWAYS.

THE SAME SHAPE CAN BE ADAPTED TO FIT QUITE DIFFERENT DECORATIVE NEEDS. HERE, FOR INSTANCE, SLENDER LEAF SHAPES AND BERRIES ADDED END-TO-END MAKE A LIVELY LINEAR DECORATION FOR THE BACK OF THE MEXICAN CHAIR.

CONTRAST PANELS BREAK UP THE SURFACE OF THE LIME GREEN BENCH AND ALSO PROVIDE AN OPPORTUNITY FOR MORE RIOTOUS COLOUR, USING THE 'TADPOLE' BORDER IN DIFFERENT COLOURWAYS. CONTRAST PANELS FRAMED WITH BORDERS ARE AN IDEAL WAY TO LIVEN UP LARGE PLAIN SURFACES.

IMPROMPTU PLACE MATS IN THE LIGHTER, BRIGHTER MEXICAN HUES DECORATE A SCRUBBED SYCAMORE TABLE TOP. NOTICE HOW THE 'TADPOLE' BORDER OUTSIDE THE PANEL TURNS INTO AN AMUSING DECORATIVE FRINGE. THE TEMPLATE COMES IN USEFUL AGAIN TO ADD A PINK RICK-RACK TRIM AROUND THE TABLE BASE. IN THE SAME INSOUCIANT SPIRIT, BANGLES OF BRILLIANT COLOUR HIGHLIGHT THE TABLE LEGS.

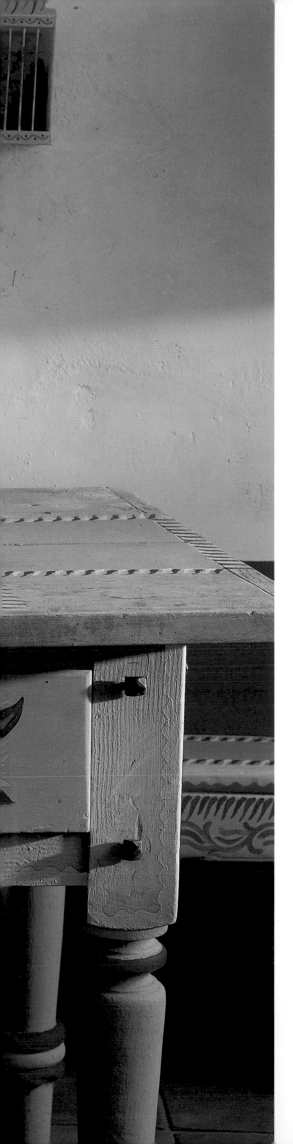

Colour works cumulatively in a setting as piquant as *salsa cruda*. If you use enough colours of the same value, the final effect is surprisingly convincing.

A FEW SQUIGGLES ARE ALL THAT IS NEEDED TO GIVE THIS TERRACOTTA POT AND PLANT HOLDER THE TRUE ACAPULCO FLAVOUR. TRY THIS SORT OF FREEHAND DECORATION AFTER YOU HAVE EXPERIMENTED WITH THE OTHER PATTERNS. YOU WILL FIND IT JUST FLOWS NATURALLY OFF YOUR BRUSH.

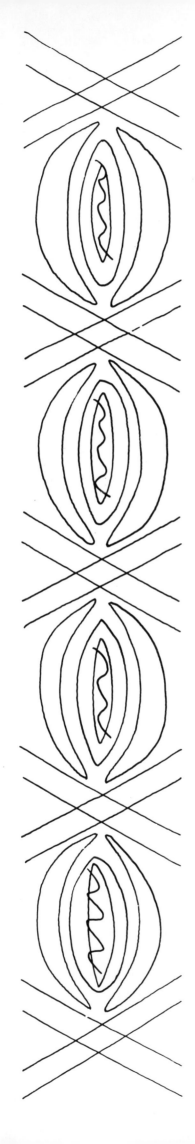

CHAPTER FOUR

Simply
AMERICAN

Friendly and folksy motifs drawn from the country traditions of the New World.

The tree of life and tulip bouquet are two of the best loved of all old motifs, appearing on painted furniture the world over. The American versions have the freshness of patchwork quilt designs and our painted daisy border is as effective as it is quick and easy to paint.

Traditional decoration is built up from many elements. Our charming bird and animal motifs can be used in pairs to create the symmetry favoured by old folk painting. The eight-pointed geometric star and corner pieces make a great panel filler.

PREPARE AND PAINT YOUR BACKGROUND

American folk painting favoured rich, earthy colours for furniture. Three typical colour mixes are shown here: traditional 'barn' red, 'Shaker' green and 'buttermilk' white.

Preparation can be minimal. Make sure surfaces are clean and non-greasy. Gloss finishes – paint or varnish – need sanding back with medium-grade sandpaper to provide a 'key' for the paint. No need to fill cracks and surface blemishes; these add character to a folk painted piece. The bedhead and commode were both painted using standard matt emulsion paints, intermixed for colour variations. Emulsion is the modern decorator's choice because it drys fast, is easy to apply, and provides an excellent surface for decoration. In this case, it also imitates the 'dry' texture of old-fashioned buttermilk paints often used by itinerant New England stencillers and painters.

IF YOU CANNOT FIND THE EXACT SHADE SHOWN HERE IN A COMMERCIAL PAINT RANGE, DARKEN A BRIGHT RED EMULSION WITH A DARKER EARTH BROWN. A BUTTERMILK OR OFF WHITE EXISTS IN MOST PAINT RANGES AND CAN BE AGED AS SHOWN HERE. MAKE A VERY DILUTED WASH BY MIXING A LITTLE OF THE EARTH BROWN SHADE WITH WATER. WITH A CLOTH WIPE THE WASH QUICKLY OVER THE BUTTERMILK AND USE A BRUSH TO PUSH IT INTO CORNERS AND CRACKS.

MOSS GREEN EMULSION WAS APPLIED IN TWO COATS TO THE VERTICAL SURFACES OF THIS PIECE. TO SUGGEST WEAR AND TEAR AND TO CREATE AN ANTIQUED EFFECT, LEADING EDGES WERE LIGHTLY ABRADED WITH MEDIUM-GRADE SAND-PAPER TO LET WOOD SHOW THROUGH. STREAKS OF BROWN-RED ADDED WITH A BRUSH OR CLOTH REINFORCE THE ILLUSION OF OLD PAINTED WOOD SHOWING THROUGH, AS SEEN HERE AND IN THE SIDE CHAIR SHOWN OPPOSITE.

STURDY SHAPES, FRIENDLY

Simple furniture pieces painted in rich country colours make an ideal background to vivid colonial-style motifs. It all adds up to a comforting, classic scene which could look as much at home in a town flat as a log cabin, anywhere, in fact, where you want to introduce a relaxed, informal look. Paint and pattern dress up a collection of unrelated pieces of furniture, some antique, some junk, and bring them together

COLOURS

harmoniously as part of an overall effect. This room was styled with a child in mind, although there is no childish whimsy to be seen. The same look would translate happily into adult environments like a kitchen or a study. Set it all off as here with cool buttermilk walls, crisp checked fabric, and, of course, a traditional calico quilt. Decorated pieces like these will become tomorrow's antiques and collectibles.

PAINTING WITH A PATTERN

Start with small repeating motifs to give yourself confidence and test out your tracing and brushwork.

Shown here are the steps involved in tracing off and painting a simple group of motifs chosen to fit a long narrow space. Points to remember: ● Use a hard lead pencil for the tracing down because this will give you a clear outline. ● Keep a clean copy of the tracing patterns – you might like to photocopy them a few times. You can then cut them up to fit awkward spaces without worrying about losing the originals. ● If you cut smaller pieces of transfer paper, be careful to leave yourself a big enough piece for the largest motif. ● All the patterns in this book were painted with fast-drying artist's acrylic colours, available in tubes from all artist's suppliers. These dry with a matt finish, and are used

TRACING DOWN AND FILLING IN

You may find it easier to cut individual motifs from your pattern sheet, and cut smaller pieces of transfer paper.

1 FIX PATTERN IN PLACE WITH MASKING TAPE. SLIP TRANSFER PAPER BENEATH. TRACE PATTERNS CAREFULLY AND FIRMLY WITH SHARP PENCIL.

2 FIND CENTRE OF SPACE. TRACE OFF HEART MOTIF. FIT BIRD PATTERN TO LEFT OF HEART. (FLIP TRACING OVER.)

5 DAISY BORDER IS PAINTED IN TWO COLOURS. USING FINE BRUSH AND COLOUR A, PAINT IN FOUR PETALS: *INCREASING BRUSH PRESSURE CREATES PETAL SHAPE AUTOMATICALLY.*

6 USING COLOUR A AND MEDIUM BRUSH, FILL IN BIRD PLUMAGE, HEART SHAPE AND TWIGS.

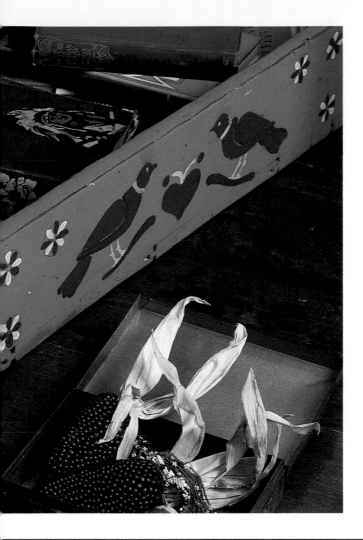

thinned with a little water to 'single cream' consistency. Use an old plate as a palette. ● Use soft watercolour brushes in different sizes to paint motifs, including one fine one for outlining. There is no need to buy expensive sable brushes – synthetic bristles or mixed hair are fine.

COLOUR RECIPES: (A) 2 PARTS CADMIUM RED, 2 PARTS ALIZARIN CRIMSON (B) WHITE WITH TOUCH OF YELLOW OCHRE

SHORT CUT FOR DAISY BORDER: YOU ONLY NEED TRACE INNER AND OUTER CIRCLE TO MARK BEGINNING AND END OF BRUSH STROKES.

3 USING RIGHT SIDE OF TRACING, TRACE OFF BIRD ON RIGHT TO MAKE PAIR.

4 COMPLETED TRACED DESIGN SHOWS ASSEMBLY OF MOTIFS READY FOR PAINTING.

7 COMPLETE DAISY USING FINE BRUSH AND COLOUR B.

8 USING COLOUR B AND FINE BRUSH, ADD BIRD'S COLLAR AND LEGS AND COMPLETE HEART.

1 THREE VIEWS OF A STAR: TRACE PATTERN, TRACE-DOWN
PAPER AND COMPLETED TRACING.

2 USE COLOUR A AND MEDIUM BRUSH TO FILL IN
ONE HALF OF GEOMETRIC TRIANGLES.

5 COLOUR B FILLS IN TRACED HORSE OUTLINE.

6 WITH FINE BRUSH, USE WHITE PAINT FOR
CONTRAST TO BRUSH IN MANE, EYE AND HOOFS.

COLOUR RECIPES

(A) WHITE AND TINY AMOUNT OF YELLOW OCHRE

(B) 2 PARTS ULTRAMARINE BLUE, 1 PART SAP GREEN

(C) ALIZARIN CRIMSON

(D) 2 PARTS CADMIUM RED, 1 PART YELLOW OCHRE

COLOUR ON A DARK BACKGROUND

Enjoy trying out different colour schemes. By adding only two more colours on a different background a whole new effect is achieved.

3 USE COLOUR B TO FILL IN OTHER HALF OF OUTER TRIANGLES. THEN USE COLOUR C FOR REMAINING INNER SEGMENTS.

4 USE COLOUR D TO CREATE FAT PETAL SHAPES IN CENTRE OF STAR.

7 WIPE OFF EXCESS PAINT ON TISSUE FOR DRY BRUSH APPLICATION OF SHADING. PRACTISE DRY BRUSH STROKES ON PAPER BEFORE APPLYING SHADE TO MOTIF.

8 BOLDNESS PAYS OFF WHEN USING DRY BRUSH STROKES.

AUTHORS' TIP
Supporting your brush hand with your other hand helps to steady your brush. This makes all the difference in achieving steady, controlled brush strokes, especially in the middle of a large painted area.

1 TREE FRAMEWORK IS FILLED IN USING COLOUR A. NOW COLOUR B BLOCKS IN HALF OF LEAF SHAPES.

2 COLOUR C DOTS IN ONE OR TWO MORE LEAVES AND PAINTS SMALL RINGS.

5 COLOUR B HAS BRUSHED IN OUTER TULIP PETALS, TAPERING EACH STROKE FINELY AT BOTH ENDS, WHILE COLOUR E FILLS IN TULIP HEART, AND FATTENS CENTRAL MOTIF.

6 USING COLOUR A, FLICK IN SMALL LEAF SHAPES AND CENTRAL STEM WITH FINE BRUSH.

AUTHORS' TIPS
Folk painting is built up with simple brush strokes, each one creating a shape. Touching a well-loaded brush straight down creates round dots. While executing a stroke, increasing downward pressure on the brush fattens the stroke, while decreasing pressure allows it to create a finer stroke shape. Practise on a piece of paper.

Having cut your teeth on the simpler patterns, it is time to have fun
with colour and the exuberant floral motifs which make such a
stunning addition to your painted furniture.

3 COLOUR D COMPLETES LEAVES TO CREATE A
BALANCED EFFECT.

4 COLOUR E HAS FILLED IN SHAPES IN MIDDLE OF TREE.
NOW COLOUR F ADDS HIGHLIGHT DOTS AND FINAL
PARTS OF LEAVES.

7 COLOUR G IS USED FOR STEMS AND TULIP
HIGHLIGHTS; EVENLY SPACED DOTS MAKE A
DRAMATIC CENTRAL MOTIF.

8 ADD YOUR OWN TOUCHES, LIKE DOTS USED HERE, TO
PRODUCE YOUR *OWN* FOLK ART.

COLOUR RECIPES

(A) EQUAL PARTS ULTRAMARINE BLUE AND SAP GREEN

(B) CADMIUM RED AND TOUCH OF CRIMSON

(C) EQUAL PARTS CADMIUM RED AND YELLOW OCHRE

(D) 2 PARTS ALIZARIN CRIMSON, 1 PART ULTRAMARINE BLUE

(E) YELLOW OCHRE AND A TOUCH OF WHITE

(F) WHITE WITH COLOUR D ADDED TO MAKE A WARM PINK

(G) WHITE WITH TOUCH OF YELLOW OCHRE

A CAVALCADE OF COLOUR

*A menagerie of folk birds and animals arranged in symmetrical pairs emphasises
the attractive shape of this antique pine bedhead.*

Colours used on the bedhead have been cleverly modified
to lighten the dark brown-red areas while adding
expressive decoration to the buttermilk headboard. Notice
how the repetition of a small motif can be used to
emphasise a structural element like the bedposts.
Wherever pairs of motifs are used, the 'flip' side of the
design has been used together with its right-side version.

YOU COULD ALWAYS LET THE COLOURS OF A TRADITIONAL
PATCHWORK QUILT SUGGEST THE COLOUR SCHEME FOR YOUR
DECORATION, OR GAIN INSPIRATION FROM AN HISTORICAL
SOURCE WHICH YOU DISCOVER YOURSELF.

CHAPTER FIVE

Sun, Moon & STARS

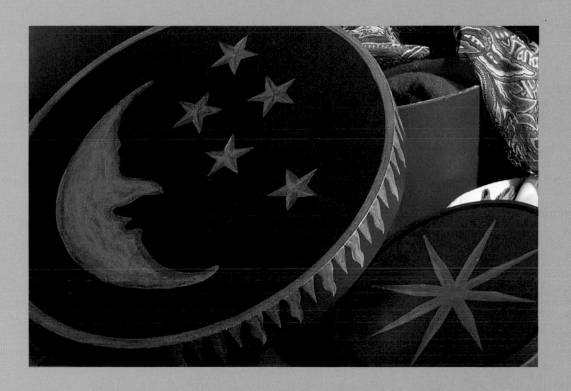

The glamour of a cosmic theme is captured by distressed metallic finishes against a rich night-sky blue.

Sun, moon and stars are among the most loved images in history. Their boldly eloquent shapes have an impact as painted decoration which is very much in line with contemporary taste. Strong moody colours suit furniture of most periods when sparked up with subdued metallic decoration.

HEAVENLY BODIES COME TO

A strong but sophisticated colour scheme - midnight blue and weathered gold - ties together a group of furniture and smaller items in many different styles. A group like this makes a very positive design statement and looks best against the plainest of painted walls. However, bare polished boards have been glamourized with our flaming star pattern, enlarged many times over using a photocopier, and coloured in with a dark woodstain for a marquetry effect. Charming tie-on cushions on our two classic

EARTH

carver chairs demonstrate how effective our painted patterns can look, dressing up cheap cotton calico. In contrast to so much gold decoration elsewhere we decided to stick to simple black and white for the fabric cushions on the chair backs.

PAINTING WITH A PATTERN

Small repeat motifs decorating a simple shape make an ideal project to test your skills.

Shown here are the steps involved in tracing off and painting two of our pattern motifs, used to enhance a plain, round wooden box.

Points to remember:
• Use a hard lead pencil for the tracing down because this will give you a clear outline.
• Keep a clean copy of the tracing patterns - you might like to photocopy them a few times, perhaps enlarging or reducing them for particular uses. You can then cut them up to fit awkward spaces without worrying about losing the originals.

• The deep blue background colour used here is a standard emulsion paint, applied over either acrylic primer or thoroughly sanded existing paint.
• Most of the patterns in this book were painted with the gold version of artists' gouache in tubes, available from all good artists' suppliers.
• Gum arabic, also available from artists' suppliers, makes a transparent tinted glaze for going over gold gouache decoration to soften and shade it. For mixing glaze colours use a plate as a palette with a dab of gum arabic in the centre and dots of gouache tinting colours around the edge.

1 FIX PATTERN IN PLACE WITH MASKING TAPE. SLIP TRANSFER PAPER BENEATH. TRACE BORDER SHAPES CAREFULLY AND FIRMLY WITH SHARP PENCIL.

2 TO EXTEND A BORDER LIKE THIS SIMPLY MOVE THE TRANSFER SHEET AND TRACING ALONG, MAKING SURE THAT THE ENDS LINK UP.

3 USING ONE HAND TO STEADY THE OTHER, AND A MEDIUM-SIZED BRUSH, THE BORDER SHAPES ARE PAINTED IN WITH COLOUR A, USED THICKLY ENOUGH TO COVER THE DARK BACKGROUND.

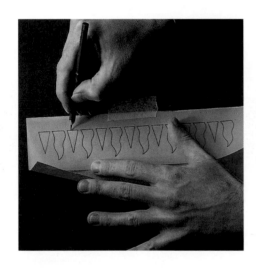

4 GLAZE B IS BRUSHED OVER ROUGHLY HALF OF EACH PAINTED GOLD SHAPE USING A DIFFERENT (CLEAN) BRUSH.

5 USE PAPER TISSUES TO BLOT UP SOME OF THE GLAZE COLOUR. THIS SPEEDS DRYING AND GIVES A MORE DELICATE EFFECT.

6 THIS SHOWS HOW MUCH GLAZE YOU WOULD EXPECT TO PICK UP BY GENTLY BLOTTING WET GLAZE WITH SOFT TISSUES.

MATERIALS CHECKLIST

WELL-SHARPENED HARD LEAD PENCIL, SCISSORS, MASKING TAPE, OLD PLATE, WATER JAR, KITCHEN PAPER OR TISSUES FOR WIPING BRUSHES, RULER OR TAPE FOR POSITIONING MOTIFS.

TUBES OF GOUACHE PAINTS IN METALLIC GOLD, RED OCHRE AND RAW SIENNA SHADES.

SMALL BOTTLE OF GUM ARABIC FOR OVERGLAZING.

TWO WATERCOLOUR BRUSHES, ONE FINE, ONE MEDIUM.

GLAZE COLOUR RECIPES:
(A) TUBE GOUACHE GOLD THINNED WITH WATER.
(B) GUM ARABIC TINTED WITH RED OCHRE.

• Use soft watercolour brushes in different sizes to outline and fill in motifs. There is no need to buy expensive sable brushes: synthetic bristles or mixed hair are fine.

1 THIS SHOWS HOW THE TRACED-DOWN STAR SHAPE IS FILLED IN WITH COLOUR A AND A FINE WATERCOLOUR BRUSH. USE YOUR FREE HAND TO STEADY THE BRUSH STROKES AS SHOWN.

2 WITH A CLEAN BRUSH, STROKE COLOUR GLAZE B DOWN ONE SIDE OF EACH STAR SPOKE, ADDING A CURVED SHADOW IN THE CENTRE FOR A DISTINCTIVE FINISH.

3 A CLOSE-UP OF THE FINISHED STAR SHOWS HOW SUBTLY THE TRANSPARENT REDDISH GLAZE WARMS UP THE FLAT GOLD GOUACHE PAINT. USING THE TECHNIQUE SHOWN ALSO LENDS A THREE-DIMENSIONAL EFFECT TO THE FLAT IMAGE.

From the simplicity of a standard metallic felt pen to the whole panoply of shading and enriching with transparent glazes, these pages suggest the variety that can be created from the same set of patterns.

1 NOTHING COULD BE EASIER THAN GOING OVER A TRACE-DOWN PATTERN WITH A COLOURED FELT PEN. IN THIS CASE THE PEN COLOUR IS GOLD, TO UNDERLINE THE SUN'S FIERY CHARACTER.

2 USING THE SAME PEN, FILL IN THE AUREOLE (RAYS) WITH GOLD, BUT LEAVE A LITTLE THREAD OF BLUE BACKGROUND SHOWING FOR LIVELINESS. HERE THE SUN'S FEATURES ARE ALSO BEING EMPHASIZED.

AUTHORS' TIP

For an even more weathered or antique look use fine wire wool pads to rub away a little of the finished image so that the blue background colour 'ghosts' through here and there.

1 USE COLOUR A AND MEDIUM BRUSH TO FILL IN THE CRESCENT MOON OUTLINE, AS PREVIOUSLY TRACED DOWN.

2 A CIRCLET OF STARS USING A REPEAT OF THE SMALL STAR PATTERN GIVES MORE IMPACT TO THE COMPOSITION.

3 GLAZE B (SEE PAGE BEFORE LAST) IS BRUSHED THINLY OVER THE ENTIRE FACE TO ENRICH AND DISTRESS THE GOLD FINISH.

4 A SECOND APPLICATION OF GLAZE B IS THEN APPLIED TO DRAMATIZE THE MOON'S EERIE PROFILE.

5 THE SAME TECHNIQUE OF GLAZING BUT WITH A SLIGHTLY STRONGER VERSION OF THE GLAZE COLOUR PICKS OUT THE STAR SHAPES TO GIVE A THREE-DIMENSIONAL FINISH.

6 THE FINISHED COMPOSITION DEMONSTRATES HOW EFFECTIVE OVERGLAZING WITH CONTRAST COLOUR IS IN GIVING WARMTH AND BRILLIANCE TO A FLAT GILT SURFACE.

1 A TAB OF MASKING TAPE HOLDS DOWN THE PATTERN OF OUR MOST COMPLEX STAR SHAPE, WHICH TAKES CORRESPONDINGLY LONGER TO TRACE DOWN AND WORK ON.

2 USING A MID-BLUE SHADE MADE BY LIGHTENING THE BACKGROUND EMULSION COLOUR WITH WHITE, THE WAVY SPOKES ARE FILLED IN FROM THEIR OUTER POINTS USING A FINE WATERCOLOUR BRUSH.

3 FILL IN THE INNERMOST POINTS AT THE OPPOSITE END OF EACH SPOKE, BRUSHING FROM THE POINT UPWARDS TO ARRIVE AT THE NEAT POINTS SHOWN HERE.

4 USE THE FINEST BRUSH TO FILL IN THE FINE POINTS OF THE TWELVE-SPOKE STAR. YOU CAN THEN USE A FATTER BRUSH TO SPEED UP PAINTING IN THE MAIN BODY OF THE MOTIF.

5 MIX A SHADE A LITTLE DARKER THAN THE MID-BLUE TO SHADE THE COMPLETED TWELVE-POINT STAR MOTIF AS SHOWN HERE.

6 THE FINISHED SUPERSTAR SHOWS HOW EFFECTIVELY THE SIMPLE TRICK OF SHADING BRINGS A FLAT IMAGE TO LIFE. FOR A CLOSER LOOK AT THE RICH HERALDIC EFFECT WHICH CAN BE ACHIEVED WITH THE SIMPLEST MEANS SEE THE ENLARGEMENT OF THE FINAL DESIGN ON THE OTHER SIDE OF THE TRACE-DOWN PATTERNS. NOTE HOW A CIRCLET OF STARS IS USED TO DRAMATIZE A CIRCULAR TABLE TOP.

Easy-to-use metallic effects like these need careful finishing to protect them against use, but also to add character to an intrinsically blank shine.

THE MANY MOODS OF METAL FINISHES

Two approaches to finishing decorative effects are shown here. One is largely protective, and makes use of a clear gloss varnish. Two to three coats of varnish, lightly rubbed down with fine wire wool, or wet-and-dry paper, give a good surface. The other uses a finishing varnish as a vehicle for antiquing colour. This mysteriously enhances the richness of a metal finish while at the same time dulling it down.

FOR A SPARKLING SURFACE WITH CONSIDERABLE RESISTANCE TO WEAR, CHOOSE A CLEAR GLOSS POLYURETHANE VARNISH. THIS VARNISH WAS CHOSEN FOR OUR THREE TABLE TOPS. NOTE, HOWEVER, THAT GOLD FELT PEN SHOULD FIRST BE 'FIXED' WITH SPRAY VARNISH TO PREVENT SMUDGING.

ADDING A LITTLE ARTISTS' TUBE OIL COLOUR TO POLYURETHANE VARNISH, IN EITHER BURNT OR RAW UMBER SHADES, MAKES A CONVENIENT ANTIQUING MEDIUM WHOSE 'DIRTYING' EFFECT SHOWS UP WELL ON THE BOX AND WASTE BIN IN THIS PICTURE.

A CONSTELLATION OF BRIGHT IDEAS

A heavenly galaxy of boxes featuring variations on our sun, moon and star motifs clusters around a hatbox painted with heraldic brilliance.

This picture proves how different the same motifs can look when either their scale or colouring is altered. A single note of bright contrast colour, like the red triangles on the hatbox, gets extra value from being surrounded by such a consistent colour scheme.

A galaxy of different effects can be wheedled from the same basic set of designs by making quite small changes, as our pictures show.

A PAIR OF TRADITIONAL, NINETEENTH-CENTURY OAK CARVERS ACQUIRE UNEXPECTED DISTINCTION WITH OUR DECORATIVE TREATMENT. THE LINING WHICH EMPHASIZES THE CHAIR SEAT, BACK AND ARMS HAS BEEN DONE EASILY AND QUICKLY BY SIMPLY DRAWING IT ON WITH TWO GOLD FELT PENS, ONE THINNER THAN THE OTHER. LINING IS ALWAYS A CHALLENGE TO AN INEXPERIENCED PAINTER AND THIS SIMPLE TRICK WILL MAKE IT MUCH LESS ALARMING. NOTE THAT ANY FELT PEN DECORATION SHOULD BE 'FIXED' WITH CLEAR SPRAY VARNISH BEFORE VARNISHING OVERALL, BECAUSE WITHOUT THIS PRECAUTION IT IS LIABLE TO SMUDGE WHEN BRUSHED OVER.

TO ARRIVE AT THEIR IMPECCABLY GLOSSY FINISH, THESE CHAIRS HAVE BEEN GIVEN THREE COATS OF CLEAR VARNISH LIGHTLY RUBBED DOWN, AND THEN A FINAL COAT OF WAX POLISH. DARK TAN SHOE POLISH ADDS PATINA AS WELL AS SHINE.

NOTHING LOOKS MORE DRAMATIC UNDERFOOT THAN A SCALED-UP STARBURST, HERE GIVEN A MARQUETRY LOOK BY PAINTING IT IN WITH DARK WOODSTAIN STRAIGHT ONTO BARE WOODEN BOARDS. THE BASIC MOTIF HAS BEEN ENLARGED MANY TIMES OVER ON A PHOTOCOPIER. THE FINAL ENLARGEMENT WAS MADE BY CUTTING OUT ONE SEGMENT AND ENLARGING AS FAR AS THE MACHINE WOULD TAKE IT ON A3 PAPER. TO REASSEMBLE THE MOTIF SIMPLY SWIVEL IT ROUND A CENTRE POINT MARKED BY A DRAWING PIN.

TO PREVENT WOODSTAIN LEAKING BEYOND THE OUTLINES, SCRIBE THEM OVER LIGHTLY WITH A SHARP CRAFT KNIFE BEFORE STAINING. APPLY THE STAIN WITH A FINE BRUSH FOR OUTLINES AND A STANDARD DECORATING BRUSH FOR INFILLING. THE DISTRESSED EFFECT COMES FROM BLOTTING STILL-WET STAIN WITH TISSUES OR CLOTH. ANY FLOOR DECORATION NEEDS PROTECTIVE SEALING; TWO TO THREE COATS OF CLEAR POLYURETHANE VARNISH HAVE BEEN USED HERE.

SEE HOW DIFFERENT THE SAME IMAGE CAN LOOK WHEN ITS COLOURS ARE REVERSED AND ITS SCALE IS ALTERED. THE SUN FACE IS SHOWN PREDOMINANTLY GOLD ON A ROUND BOX TOP, BUT ON THE LITTLE WALL SCONCES, HE HAS GONE INTO ECLIPSE, WITH A DARK FACE ENCIRCLED BY FIERY SPOKES. BOTH BACKGROUND COLOURS HAVE BEEN ENRICHED WITH FURTHER LAYERS OF TRANSPARENT GLAZES TO SOFTEN THE CONTRAST BETWEEN BOLD IMAGE AND PLAIN GROUND, SINCE THERE IS OTHERWISE A TENDENCY FOR THE DECORATION TO 'JUMP OUT' RESTLESSLY.

CHAPTER SIX

Classic COLLECTION

Serene and timeless, the motifs in our Classic Collection add repose to a contemporary setting.

Our selection of borders dating back to classical times can be used in a variety of combinations with our quartet of handsome motifs inspired by Greek sculpture and pottery to lend colour and interest to contemporary or even junk pieces of furniture. Against the dark background colours currently fashionable for interiors, the rich lustre of metallic paints shows up with sumptuous effect.

THE MUTED GLEAM OF ANTIQUE

The spirit of classicism is one of disciplined elegance: discreet rather than flamboyant. In this boldly coloured interior, our Classic Collection motifs give an unobtrusive richness to a disparate collection of pieces. It is the details that score here. Note how

strikingly the painted borders set off the coloured picture mounts, and how a discreet use of gold lining and ornament gives status to a very ordinary small dining table. Gilt wreaths dramatize the seats of plain painted wooden chairs, while the matching

GOLD

carver sports a glamorous flowering lyre. For contrast, compare the metallic effects with the same designs painted in white on the tray table. Two borders combined with lining make something quite splendid from a deep, moulded mirror frame,

glimpsed hanging just above. Strongly coloured walls and the black woodwork dado rail create a dramatic decorative scheme with an Arts and Crafts atmosphere that is currently one of the top favourites with younger interior designers.

PAINTING WITH A PATTERN

Small repeat motifs decorating a simple shape make an ideal project to test your skills.

Our stylized fleur-de-lys motif makes a reassuringly easy project to start with, as well as adding considerable visual impact to the wooden jardiniere.

Points to remember:
- Use a hard lead pencil for the tracing down because this will give you a clear outline.
- Keep a clean copy of the tracing patterns - you might like to photocopy them a few times. You can then cut them up to fit awkward spaces without worrying about losing the originals.
- Background colours throughout this chapter

were achieved with standard emulsion paints, applied over either acrylic primer or thoroughly sanded existing paint.
- Many of the designs were painted with the gold version of artists' gouache in tubes, available from all good artists' suppliers. Artists' acrylic tube colour, fast-drying and convenient, was used for painting in coloured details. Gilt lining becomes simplicity itself done with a ruler and a gold felt pen.
- The beauty of these timeless motifs is that they somehow look appropriate on most simply shaped pieces from any period. Interpreting them in gold

 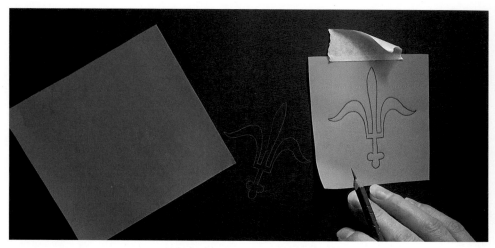

1 A TAB OF MASKING TAPE HOLDS THE TRACING PATTERN IN PLACE OVER THE BLUE TRANSFER PAPER, WHILE THE PATTERN IS TRACED DOWN FIRMLY WITH A WELL-SHARPENED HARD LEAD PENCIL.

2 THIS SHOWS THE COMPLETED MOTIF TRANSFERRED TO THE PAINTED SURFACE USING OUR BLUE TRANSFER PAPER. TO MAKE THE JOB EASIER, USE A SMALL SQUARE OF TRANSFER PAPER THAT HAS BEEN CUT TO THE DIMENSIONS OF THE MOTIF.

3 USING A MEDIUM-SIZED WATERCOLOUR BRUSH AND COLOUR A, FILL IN THE FLEUR-DE-LYS PETALS STARTING AT THEIR EXTREMITIES FOR A CLEAN AND DECISIVE POINT. PRACTISE THIS BRUSHWORK IF YOU LIKE ON A PIECE OF PAPER FIRST.

4 WITH A CLEAN BRUSH DIPPED IN COLOUR B, HIGHLIGHT THE PETALS AS SHOWN. USE YOUR FREE HAND TO SUPPORT THE PAINTING HAND WHILE YOU WORK.

5 MORE GOLD GOUACHE IS USED TO HIGHLIGHT THE TREFOIL SHAPE AT THE BASE OF OUR MOTIF.

MATERIALS CHECKLIST

WELL-SHARPENED HARD LEAD PENCIL, SCISSORS, MASKING TAPE, OLD
PLATE, WATER JAR, KITCHEN PAPER OR TISSUES FOR WIPING BRUSHES,
RULER OR TAPE FOR POSITIONING MOTIFS.

ACRYLIC TUBE COLOURS IN VENETIAN RED, ALIZARIN CRIMSON AND
HOOKER'S GREEN.

GOLD FELT PEN.

GOUACHE TUBE COLOUR IN GOLD.

TWO WATERCOLOUR BRUSHES, ONE FINE, ONE MEDIUM.

LENGTH OF BULL-NOSED MOULDING FOR LINING WITH GOLD FELT PEN
OR FINE BRUSH.

COLOUR RECIPES:

(A) ALIZARIN CRIMSON MIXED WITH A VERY LITTLE VENETIAN RED.
(B) GOUACHE GOLD THINNED WITH WATER.

against dark paintwork creates an effect reminiscent
of Empire furniture with its severe shapes brightened
by ormolu, brass stringing and touches of gold leaf.
• Use soft watercolour brushes in different sizes to
outline and fill in motifs. There is no need to buy
expensive sable brushes - synthetic bristles or mixed
hair are fine.

1 THIS SHOWS THE ANTHEMION DESIGN
MOTIF TRACED OFF USING BLUE TRANSFER
PAPER. EVEN AGAINST A DARK BACKGROUND
LIKE THE ONE HERE, THE OUTLINES ARE QUITE
CLEAR ENOUGH TO REGISTER.

2 A GOLD FELT PEN MAKES A DELIGHTFULLY
SIMPLE PAINTING TOOL, AS SHOWN HERE.
NOTE HOW A WHISKER OF BACKGROUND
COLOUR LEFT VISIBLE GIVES VIVACITY TO THE
STYLIZED PETAL SHAPES.

3 SIGNING OFF THE COMPLETED MOTIF. THE
ANTHEMION SHAPE IS A TRADITIONAL
ORNAMENT OFTEN USED IN COMBINATION
WITH GOLD LINES TO DECORATE THE CORNERS
OF PIECES OF FURNITURE.

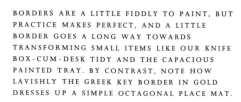

BORDERS ARE A LITTLE FIDDLY TO PAINT, BUT PRACTICE MAKES PERFECT, AND A LITTLE BORDER GOES A LONG WAY TOWARDS TRANSFORMING SMALL ITEMS LIKE OUR KNIFE BOX-CUM-DESK TIDY AND THE CAPACIOUS PAINTED TRAY. BY CONTRAST, NOTE HOW LAVISHLY THE GREEK KEY BORDER IN GOLD DRESSES UP A SIMPLE OCTAGONAL PLACE MAT.

COLOUR RECIPES:
(A) GOUACHE WHITE THINNED WITH WATER.
(B) ALIZARIN CRIMSON MIXED WITH A VERY LITTLE VENETIAN RED.

1 A BULL-NOSED (ROUNDED) MOULDING MAKES PAINTING A FINE STRAIGHT LINE EASIER, STEADYING THE BRUSH HAND AND PREVENTING PAINT SMUDGING AS IT MIGHT IF YOU USED A FLAT RULER. USE A FINE BRUSH FOR THIS WITH COLOUR A.

2 HAVING ESTABLISHED THE CENTRE LINE, THE SAME COLOUR AND BRUSH ARE USED TO FILL IN WHITE DOTS - WHICH REPRESENT BERRIES - BEFORE CHANGING TO A CLEAN BRUSH AND COLOUR B TO FILL IN THE TRACED-DOWN LEAF SHAPES.

3 THE FINISHED BORDER HAS A CRISP ELEGANCE THAT HAS MADE IT A FAVOURITE DECORATIVE DEVICE SINCE THE DAYS OF CLASSICAL GREEK VASE PAINTING.

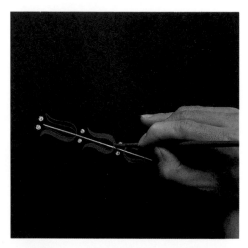

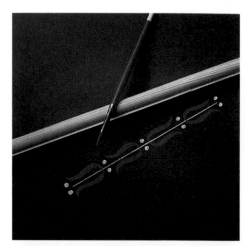

1 THE BEVELLED EDGE OF A STANDARD PLASTIC SET SQUARE WORKS WELL AS AN AID TO LINING WITH A GOLD FELT PEN. TRY TO MAINTAIN EVEN PRESSURE, TAKING SPECIAL CARE OVER 'JOINS'. PRACTISE FIRST ON A SHEET OF PAPER TO GET THE HANG OF IT.

2 WITH THE OUTER LINES IN PLACE, DRAWING OUT THE REST OF THIS CLASSIC SCROLL BORDER IS RELAXING AND SPEEDY, SIMPLY A CASE OF 'GOING OVER' THE TRACED-DOWN DESIGN.

3 THE GOLD FELT PEN AGAIN IS AN IDEAL TOOL FOR EXECUTING THIS VARIANT ON THE SCROLL BORDER MOTIF. BUT, AS BEFORE, IT ALWAYS HELPS TO REHEARSE THE MOVEMENTS FIRST ON ROUGH PAPER BECAUSE CONFIDENCE BREEDS FLUENCY.

OUR TRANSFER APPROACH ALLOWS BEGINNERS TO ACHIEVE LIVELY BUT RELAXED EXECUTION OF TRADITIONAL BORDER MOTIFS LIKE THE ONES SHOWN ON THIS PAGE. NOTE: ANY GOLD FELT PEN DECORATION NEEDS 'FIXING' WITH SPRAY VARNISH BEFORE ANY FURTHER SEALING OR VARNISHING.

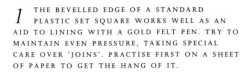

1 THE CELEBRATED GREEK KEY BORDER, STILL THE MOST ARRESTING OF GEOMETRIC MOTIFS, BEGINS HERE WITH TRACING DOWN THE BORDER ELEMENTS THROUGH BLUE TRANSFER PAPER USING A SHARP PENCIL.

2 FILLING IN THE DESIGN AS SHOWN HERE, WITH SHORT DASHES AND RETAINING OUTER GUIDELINES, SPEEDS UP THE REPETITIVE ELEMENT WHICH IS AN INEVITABLE PART OF HAND-PAINTED BORDERS.

3 THE FINAL AND FUN BIT, YET AGAIN, CONSISTS OF FILLING IN THE MISSING ELEMENTS WITH THE GOLD FELT PEN USING THE BLUE TRACINGS AS A GUIDE.

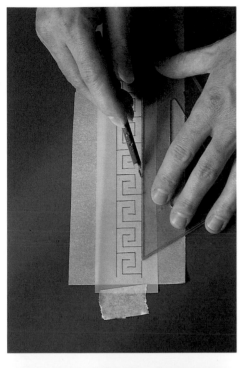

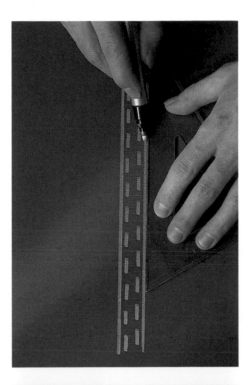

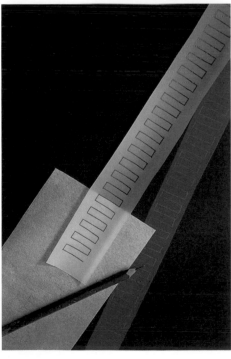

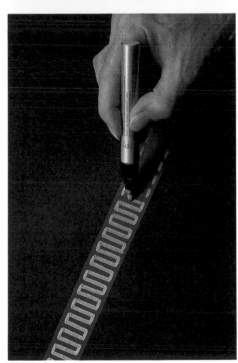

1 A CONTINUOUS GOLD LINE MAKES A HANDSOME AND EFFECTIVE BORDER DEVICE, ESPECIALLY STRIKING WHEN, AS HERE, IT IS SET OFF BY A CONTRASTING PAINTED BAND, USING COLOUR MIX B.

2 FOR SPEED AND ACCURACY, USE THE BULL-NOSED MOULDING TO GUIDE THE SHORT DASH STROKES. YOU NEED TO MAINTAIN A STRAIGHT LINE IF THIS SIMPLE MOTIF IS TO KEEP TO THE STRAIGHT AND NARROW.

3 WITH GUIDELINES ESTABLISHED, IT IS EASY AND STRAIGHTFORWARD TO FILL IN THE MISSING SECTIONS OF THE BORDER MOTIF TO CREATE A CONTINUOUS LINE. THE FELT PEN TECHNIQUE IS ESPECIALLY HELPFUL FOR EXECUTING DESIGNS WITH LOTS OF ANGLES.

Two of the most poetic images of antiquity - the laurel wreath and the flowering lyre - make superb decorations for a space where a strong shape is needed like the chair seats shown here.

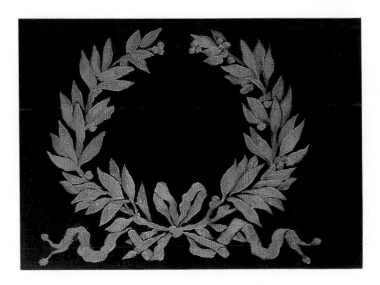

COLOUR RECIPE:
(A) GOLD GOUACHE TUBE COLOUR.

1 MEDIUM AND FINE BRUSHES ARE BEING USED WITH COLOUR A TO FILL IN THE LEAVES AND BERRIES OF THE WREATH MOTIF. NOTE HOW THE DARK BACKGROUND 'GHOSTING' THROUGH CONTRIBUTES TO THE SUBTLY SHADED EFFECT.

2 THE WREATH HAS BEEN BLOCKED IN LEAVING PLENTY OF DARK SHADOWING. NOW CAREFULLY PAINT IN THE ELABORATELY FLUTTERING BOW RIBBONS USING THE FINE BRUSH.

3 STRENGTHEN HIGHLIGHTS THROUGHOUT THE MOTIF BY STIPPLING MORE PAINT ONTO LEAVES AND RIBBON WITH THE POINT OF THE BRUSH, CREATING A DELICATE AND CONTROLLED BUILD-UP OF COLOUR.

4 THE FINISHED MOTIF HAS A ROMANTIC, PAINTERLY QUALITY THAT WOULD ENHANCE ANY SUITABLY CLASSICAL PIECE. IMAGINE IT ON A CHAIR BACK, CENTRING A ROUND TABLE TOP OR ON A DOOR PANEL.

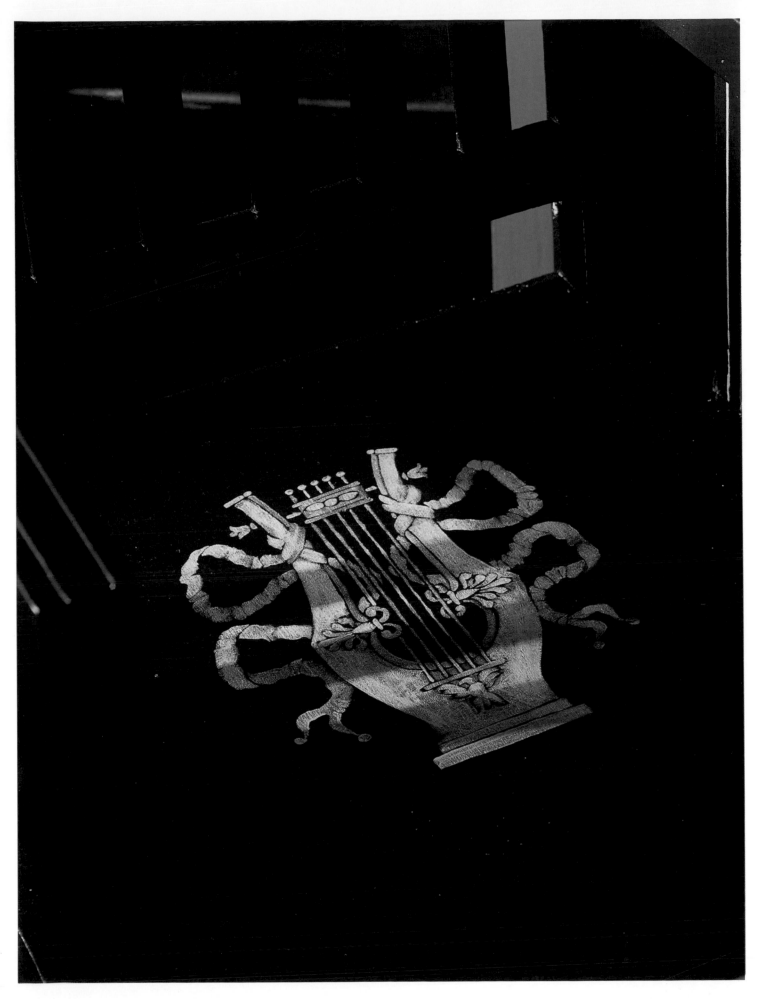

OUR VERSION OF THE NEO-
CLASSICAL FLOWERING LYRE MOTIF
MAKES ANOTHER STRIKING AND
GLAMOROUS ORNAMENT, STRONG
ENOUGH TO STAND ALONE WITH
PERHAPS A LITTLE GILT LINEWORK
AS A FRAME.

Glossy dark colours and painted ornament combine for Empire elegance.

PAINT PROTECTION

The reason designers keep going back to the classical vocabulary of ornament is that these motifs manage to be both adaptable and timeless. Use them scaled up for drama, or discreetly, as here, adding style and shapeliness to simple pieces. Details like the ones highlighted are quick to do with our transfers but they create a strong visual link and can be the making of a room.

PIECES THAT GET A LOT OF USE AND WEAR LIKE THIS TABLE NEED THOROUGH FINISHING TO KEEP PAINT AND DECORATION IN GOOD SHAPE. APPLY AT LEAST TWO COATS OF CLEAR GLOSS POLYURETHANE VARNISH. RUB THE FINAL COAT WITH FINE WET-AND-DRY ABRASIVE PAPER DIPPED INTO WATER. THIS GIVES A LUXURIOUSLY SILKY FINISH WITH GOOD PROTECTION FOR WHAT IS UNDERNEATH.

ALWAYS GIVE GOLD FELT PEN WORK A QUICK BLAST OF SPRAY VARNISH TO 'FIX' IT BEFORE GOING ON TO FURTHER TREATMENTS; OTHERWISE THERE IS A RISK OF SMUDGING THE PEN WORK WHEN THE SURFACE IS BRUSHED.

SPLENDID EXAMPLES OF THE ELEGANCE OF CLASSIC BORDERS TRANSFORMING THE MOST BASIC SHAPES: THIS SET OF DARK GREEN PLACE MATS AND THE SIDES OF A WELL-PROPORTIONED TRAY DON THE GREEK KEY AND SCROLL MOTIFS. ON PIECES LIKE THESE, LIKELY TO BE SUBJECTED TO HEAVY DAILY USE, CAREFUL AND THOROUGH VARNISHING IS ESPECIALLY IMPORTANT TO PROTECT YOUR WORK.

DECORATIVE DETAILS THAT TRANSFORM A ROOM

Use our classic motifs to give a touch of class quickly and easily to all sorts of household items.

THIS STRIKING QUARTET OF FRAMED PRINTS SHOWS HOW EFFECTIVELY FELT PEN WORK CAN UPGRADE THE CHEAPEST FRAMES. THE SECRET IS IN THE PICTURE MOUNTS: PLAIN CARD IN BLACK AND WHITE, BUT GIVEN TERRIFIC IMPACT BY RICHLY COLOURED BANDS OF DECORATION ENCLOSING THE PICTURE SPACE. TO SUGGEST SOME OF THE POTENTIAL FOR VARIATION, COMPARE THE DECORATION ON THE TWO SMALLER FRAMES, WHERE THE IDENTICAL GREEK KEY BORDER IS GIVEN A QUITE DIFFERENT LOOK BY ALTERING THE BACKGROUND COLOURS AND USING A BLACK FELT PEN ON ONE AND A GOLD PEN ON THE OTHER. WHEN THE FRAMING LOOKS THIS DISTINGUISHED AND CONFIDENT, YOU CAN GET AWAY WITH MERE PHOTOCOPIES OF PICTURES, AS WE DID HERE.

A STRONG COLOUR SCHEME LIKE THIS POMPEIIAN-INSPIRED USE OF WARM DARK COLOURS TEMPERED WITH BLACK GIVES AN INTERIOR IMMENSE CHARACTER. BUT TERRACOTTA WALLS COULD FEEL CLAUSTROPHOBIC WITHOUT PICTURES TO CREATE 'WINDOWS' WITHIN THE WALL SURFACE. OUR FOUR PICTURES HAVE BEEN HUNG SYMMETRICALLY ACROSS THE WALL. THE PALE MOUNTS ON THE LARGER FRAMES BALANCE THE BLACK PAINTED FIREPLACE BELOW, AND THE COLOURED BANDS ON ALL FOUR MOUNTS PICK UP AND ENHANCE COLOURS ALREADY PRESENT ELSEWHERE IN THE ROOM.

ADAPT YOUR DECORATIVE IDEAS TO THE
SHAPE AND STYLE OF YOUR PAINTED
PIECES. THIS UPRIGHT CARVER-STYLE
CHAIR HAS BEEN DECORATED TO FOCUS
INTEREST ON THE BACK AND SEAT. THE
GLAMOROUS LYRE MOTIF ON THE SEAT IS
BALANCED BY SIMPLE GILT LINES AND
DOTS ON THE BACK UPRIGHTS, AND A
SMALL SNIPPET OF A BORDER DESIGN ON
THE FRONT RAIL.

THIS REPRO VERSION OF A CLASSIC PIECE OF
FURNITURE – THE TEA OR DRINKS TRAY ON A
FOLDING STAND – HAS BEEN GIVEN A CHIC
PERIOD LOOK BY PAINTING IT GLOSSY BLACK
AND UNDERLINING ITS SHAPE WITH
DECORATION IN PLAIN WHITE.

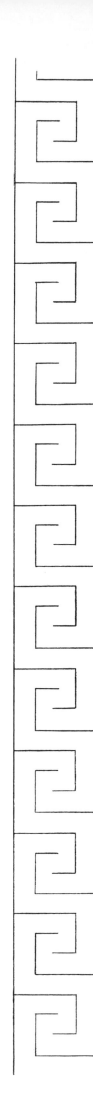

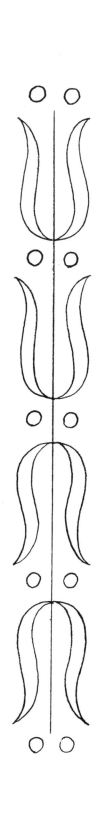

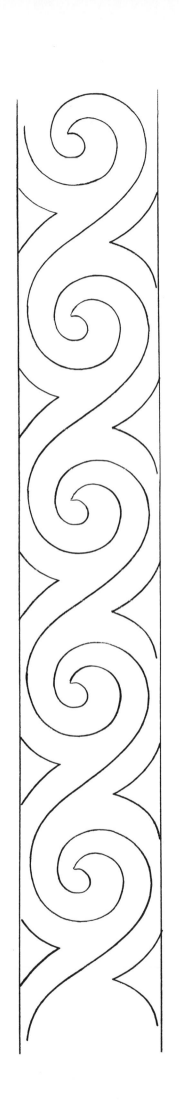

CHAPTER SEVEN

English ROSE

Transparent watercolour captures the fragile beauty of England's 'unofficial' rose. The wild rose clusters and floral motifs that make up our English Rose collection are a natural choice for bedroom suites, whether or not you live in the country. Choose a pale base colour and add a profusion of roses – clusters, arching sprays, a single bloom – to bring new charm and coherence to all your painted furniture from a folding screen to a trinket box.

Watercolour paints give this enchanting set of motifs something of the fine clarity of old botanical prints. And, contrary to popular belief, are a medium that even beginners can handle with success following the detailed instructions that follow.

ROSES, ROSES, RIOTING

Set off by rose-pink walls and touches of polished mahogany, our English Rose motifs create a rustic bower on everything they touch, unifying a set of disparate pieces of furniture from many periods. The curvaceous pine bedstead and washstand get the most elaborate treatment, in vivid colours picked up by bands of bright rosy pink against an ivory background. You could easily use this approach to lend a new lease of life to a set of pine furniture that is beginning to look dreary. As a base colour, use ivory matt emulsion over acrylic primer, smoothed over with fine sandpaper, or vary the effect by introducing another pale shade on some of the pieces, like the bedside cupboard and

E V E R Y W H E R E

charming plant stand, which are base-coated in the palest of greens. Note that transparent watercolour paints can only be used over pale backgrounds. Anything darker will show through the decoration, altering the effect unless you are prepared to undertake a complex 'whiting out' process first. The tall screen, made up simply of panels of

medium-density-fibreboard, gets the most watery, painterly treatment: rose clusters clambering up the panels and centring the cut-out tops. With such a strong thematic link between the painted pieces, the remaining items can be of the simplest origins, like the Lloyd Loom chair shown here, some pale dhurry rugs, or a faded quilt.

PAINTING WITH A PATTERN

With our patterns to guide you, and photographs to inspire you, professional-looking decoration is a breeze, even for beginners.

• Shown here are the steps involved in tracing off and colouring in the pretty border design shown on the washstand where it 'frames' more complex floral motifs. In two softly contrasting 'rosy' colours, pink and green, this simple design gives useful practice in handling the watercolour medium.
• Throughout we used artists' gouache tube colours, a convenient watercolour medium favoured by professionals, and mixed them with gum arabic, a clear medium sold by artists' suppliers, varying the amount of gum arabic according to the transparency or vividness required.
• Gum arabic makes the paint easier to control, giving smoothness to your brushwork.
• Use soft watercolour brushes, in sizes from fine to medium. There is no need to buy expensive sable brushes — synthetic bristles or mixed hair are fine.

Note: Transparent watercolour paint is inherently more fragile than emulsion and needs 'fixing' on completion of decoration, before you proceed to further varnishing, antiquing etc. All the decoration in this series was fixed with a rapid blast of spray varnish, available from artists' suppliers.

1 THE BORDER MOTIF OF INTERTWINED RIBBONS IS TRACED DOWN WITH A SHARP PENCIL THROUGH THE TRANSFER PAPER. CUTTING BOTH THE TRACING AND TRANSFER PAPER TO SIZE SPEEDS UP THE WORK.

2 THIS SHOWS HOW ONE COMPLETED SECTION IS MARRIED UP TO THE NEXT BEFORE CONTINUING THE TRACING PROCESS.

3 USING COLOUR A AND A FLAT BRUSH, THE PALE GREEN RIBBON IS FILLED IN. NOTE HOW THE SPARE HAND IS BEING USED TO SUPPORT AND GUIDE THE PAINTING HAND.

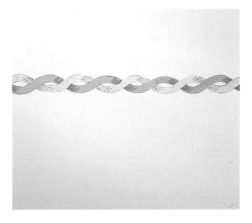

4 WITH COLOUR B, AND THE SAME BRUSH RINSED AND DRIED, THE SECOND RIBBON IS ADDED, SECTION BY SECTION.

5 A PAINTERLY TOUCH WHICH BRINGS THE BORDER TO LIFE: USING THE SAME BRUSH BUT A STRONGER SHADE OF GREEN (MORE GOUACHE, LESS GUM ARABIC) DEEPEN THE GREEN AS SHOWN, USING A PECKY MOTION TO GIVE A RUN OF LITTLE CROSS-HATCHED LINES RATHER THAN A FLUID STROKE.

6 THE SAME PROCESS HAS BEEN REPEATED IN COLOUR B FOR THE PINK RIBBON. THIS USE OF THE BRUSH GIVES A SUGGESTION OF CRISP FABRIC SUCH AS RIBBON RATHER THAN MERE ROUNDED 'WORMS' OF COLOUR.

1 FILL IN THE SMALLEST OF THE THREE SCROLL SHAPES THAT MAKE UP THIS STYLIZED ROPE BORDER USING COLOUR A AND A MEDIUM-SIZED WATERCOLOUR BRUSH.

2 COLOUR C AND A FINER BRUSH ARE USED TO PLACE THE SLENDER CALLIGRAPHIC FLOURISHES UNDER THE PREVIOUS SHAPES.

3 USING COLOUR D AND THE SAME BRUSH, RINSED AND DRIED, A TWIN OF THE PREVIOUSLY COMPLETED SHAPE IS BRUSHED ALONGSIDE. ULTRA-SIMPLE DESIGNS LIKE THIS NEED PRECISE EXECUTION, SO PRACTISE THE BRUSHWORK TILL YOU FEEL EASY WITH IT.

Having learnt how to handle and enjoy this attractive medium, and how to use the tonal range it offers, you are now ready to tackle a more ambitious project like our decorated screen. If possible paint each panel separately, laying it flat on a table or propping it at an angle if you find this easier.

1 THIS SHOWS THE TRACED-DOWN FLORAL MOTIF BEING FILLED IN WITH COLOUR E USING A MEDIUM-FINE WATERCOLOUR BRUSH. AFTER FILLING IN THE LEAVES WITH THE PALER SHADE, WORK A LITTLE MORE GOUACHE INTO THE MIXTURE FOR EMPHASIS.

2 MORE LEAVES AND A FEW STALKS HAVE NOW BEEN ADDED TO BUILD UP THE MOTIF. NOTE THE EFFECT YOU SHOULD BE AIMING FOR: FINE, DARK ACCENTS ON A PREVAILINGLY WATERY BASE COLOUR.

3 COLOUR F IS USED BOTH TO PAINT IN THE THICKER STEMS AND TO SOFTEN AND WARM THE LEAVES HERE AND THERE.

7 THE ROSES AT LAST, USING QUITE DIFFERENT COLOURS, AND A CLEVER TECHNIQUE BORROWED FROM SCANDINAVIAN FOLK 'ROSEMALING' PAINTERS. A ROUND BRUSH AND A FLAT BRUSH ARE NEEDED.

8 PRACTISE MAKING PETAL SHAPES WITH THE ROUND BRUSH ON THE MIXING PLATE, USING THE FLAKE WHITE TINGED EVER SO SLIGHTLY WITH ALIZARIN ROSE MADDER.

9 USING THE PETAL TECHNIQUE YOU PRACTISED ON THE PLATE, NOW ADD THE CRISP PINK FRILL EDGING TO THE PETALS FILLED IN WITH WHITE.

4 USE COLOUR F AND A FINE BRUSH TO WASH IN SOME LIVELY VEINING ON THE LEAVES, TO CRISP UP THE STEMS, AND TO ADD A TOUCH OF EXPRESSIVENESS TO THE DESIGN.

5 A LITTLE FLAKE WHITE ADDED TO COLOUR F IS USED TO SOFTEN AND HIGHLIGHT THE LEAF SHAPES HERE AND THERE.

6 COLOUR G STRIKES A WARM NOTE ALONG THE ROSE STEMS FOR A TOUCH OF REALISM WHICH 'LIFTS' THE WHOLE DESIGN.

10 THE SECOND ROSE IS NOW ALMOST COMPLETE, PAINTED USING EXACTLY THE SAME TECHNIQUE.

11 THE GOLDEN HEARTS ARE BRUSHED IN WITH COLOUR H, AND THEN BROUGHT TO LIFE WITH TINY DOTS OF COLOUR J DROPPED IN WITH THE POINT OF A FINE BRUSH.

12 THE SAME COLOURS ARE USED TO FILL IN BUDS AND HALF-OPENED BLOOMS, AGAIN MAKING USE OF THE FLAT BRUSH TECHNIQUE TO SHADE THE PETALS DELICATELY.

COLOUR RECIPES

(E) PERMANENT GREEN DEEP PLUS ULTRAMARINE AND A LITTLE FLAKE WHITE

(F) RAW SIENNA AND A TRACE OF COLOUR E

(G) RAW SIENNA PLUS ALIZARIN ROSE MADDER

(H) YELLOW OCHRE PLUS FLAKE WHITE

(J) RAW SIENNA

A bit more creative leeway comes in arranging various of the pattern elements to form the clambering border of leaves and flowers which runs up both sides of each screen panel. Use the same colours, in the same graded tones, as for the central cluster on the preceding page.

1 THIS SHOWS HOW THE BORDER IS BUILT UP BY CUTTING AROUND SEPARATE PATTERN ELEMENTS AND TRYING OUT VARIOUS ARRANGEMENTS THAT LOOK NATURAL.

3 AS BEFORE, THE LEAF SPRAYS ARE WASHED IN USING COLOUR E, BEFORE ADDING FINE EMPHASIS WITH COLOUR F. WITHOUT BEING SLAVISHLY NATURALISTIC, A VARIETY OF SUBTLE COLOUR IS AIMED AT.

4 THE DEFINING PROCESS CONTINUES SLOWLY ACROSS THE WHOLE MOTIF, CREATING A BALANCED UNIVERSALITY OF TONE. TRY TO AVOID MONOTONOUS PERFECTION – MAKE SOME LEAVES MORE EMPHATIC, OTHERS MORE YELLOW AND MISTY LOOKING.

6 WORKING FROM LEFT TO RIGHT (IF YOU ARE RIGHT HANDED), ADD THE ROSES AND BUDS. USE THE FLAT BRUSH AND POINTED BRUSH AND THE TECHNIQUE OF SHADING PREVIOUSLY SHOWN.

7 NOW THAT ALMOST ALL THE FLOWERS ARE COMPLETE THE RICHNESS OF THE OVERALL EFFECT IS APPARENT. NOTE, AS BEFORE, HOW THE FREE HAND IS USED AS A 'REST'.

2 HAVING FIXED ON A 'MOVEMENT' TO FOLLOW, THE ELEMENTS OF THE BORDER PATTERN ARE TRACED DOWN THROUGH THE BLUE TRANSFER PAPER ON TO THE PIECE OF FURNITURE.

5 USING A FINE BRUSH, NOW WORK IN THE STEMS AND STALKS TO GIVE THE MOTIF STRUCTURE, USING COLOUR F.

8 THE YELLOW CENTRES HAVE BEEN ADDED AND NOW A FINE BRUSH AND DOTS OF COLOUR J ARE USED TO PAINT IN THE STAMENS, THE FINAL DETAILS IN THE COMPOSITION.

A POT-POURRI OF DECORATIVE IDEAS

Posies of roses gain pungency from simple decorative 'framing'.

These detail pictures illustrate how much mileage can be obtained from one set of floral motifs, simply by varying the intensity of colour and tone, changing the background colour, or by re-arranging the posies and sprays themselves to create shapes that fill and dramatize a particular space, such as the washstand back and top, a cupboard door panel or our sweepingly curvaceous bedhead. Time spent jigging your motifs about on the surface for the best effect is never wasted.

A CHARMINGLY SIMPLE BEDSIDE CUPBOARD GAINS A NEW DIMENSION WHEN PAINTED THE PALEST OF GREENS, WITH THE TOP AND BASE IN DARK GREEN AND A DARK GREEN LINE USED TO 'FRAME' THE DECORATED DOOR PANEL.

THE WATERCOLOURS HERE ARE MORE VIVID AND JUICIER, ALLOWING A LIVELIER ACCENTING OF THE WHOLE PIECE WITH BANDS OF MOULDING PICKED OUT IN VIVID PINK. NOTE HOW CLEVERLY THE ROSE CLUSTERS HAVE BEEN SYMMETRICALLY ARRANGED TO ECHO THE CUT-OUT PROFILE OF THE BEDSTEAD ITSELF.

THE FLOWER ARRANGER'S ART

By re-arranging, pruning, or reversing patterns, a few designs can be tailored to fit and glamourize all those blank surfaces crying out for imaginative decoration.

Any really pale colour will make a suitable base coat for our English Rose collection, whether it's the palest pink, blue, yellow, cream, green or ivory. Make sure the base colour is truly opaque (at least two coats) and well smoothed with wet-and-dry paper because such fine work demands a well-prepared ground. Spray varnish each decorative passage on completion for extra protection. Lining and picking out should use the same gouache and gum arabic combination, in harmonizing colours, but don't overdo this. A final 'antiquing' finish, using matt or eggshell polyurethane varnish lightly tinted with oil tube colour (oily varnish needs oily tints), will soften and integrate the whole scheme, and make it look even more natural.

WHAT COULD BE PRETTIER THAN A BED OF MINIATURE INDOOR ROSES CONTAINED IN A PLANTER LIKE THIS? THE PIECE COULD BE FRENCH, AND THE REGULARLY REPEATED MOTIF, 'TWISTED RIBBON' BORDERS AND 'PICKING OUT' OF THE TURNED LEGS ALL CONTRIBUTE TO ITS FRIVOLOUS CHARM.

VAGUELY HEART-SHAPED ARRANGEMENTS OF THE BASIC MOTIF NICELY EMPHASIZE THE CURVES OF THE CUT-OUT PINE BEDHEAD AND FOOT, WHILE A VIVID PINK 'PICKS OUT' DETAILS OF TURNED MOULDING ON THE LEGS AND POSTS.

ROSES, OLD AND NEW, SEEM TO
COMPLEMENT ONE ANOTHER IN
DECORATION AS EFFORTLESSLY AS
THEY DO IN NATURE. HERE, OLD
PAINTED CERAMICS AND TODAY'S
WATERCOLOUR PAINTING ON THE
VICTORIAN WASHSTAND EMBRACE
LIKE OLD FRIENDS.

Can you ever have too much of a good thing? Half the fun of our transfer patterns lies in the ease with which they can be adapted. Use them not just to dress up larger items of furniture but also to glorify little things — such as trays and boxes — for a thought-through effect which makes a room look cherished.

PS: Personalized 'trifles' like these make brilliant gifts - just add an initial or two.

FLOWERY BREAKFAST TRAYS AND AN ENCHANTING HEART-SHAPED BOX ARE PRETTY ENOUGH TO TAKE THE STING OUT OF WAKING UP. IN THEIR SMALL COMPASS THEY ILLUSTRATE HOW THE SAME MOTIFS CAN BE USED TO DIFFERENT EFFECT, LOOSELY OR FORMALLY, IN VIVID COLOURS OR AS FADED AS THE LAST ROSE OF SUMMER.

A MELTINGLY PRETTY EARLY-MORNING VIGNETTE CONSISTS OF NOTHING MORE THAN ONE OF OUR ROSE-WREATHED TRAYS NUDGED UP TO THE PAINTED BEDHEAD.

A CONVINCING DEMONSTRATION ON A
SMALL SCALE OF THE IMPORTANCE OF
'FRAMING' EVEN (OR ESPECIALLY) THE
MOST ETHEREAL STYLE OF PAINTED
DECORATION. LINING ON THE BOX AND
WASHSTAND, IN PINK AND GREEN, HOLDS
THE WHOLE SCHEME TOGETHER. PRACTISE
THIS FIRST ON PAPER WITH A FINE BRUSH.
BEGINNERS' LINES MAY WOBBLE A
FRACTION, BUT AIM FOR A CARELESS
HANDPAINTED EFFECT, WHICH IS
ALWAYS MUCH MORE PREFERABLE TO
FACTORY-FINISHED EXACTNESS.

THE SOFTER, MORE WATERY RENDERING OF
THE ENGLISH ROSE PATTERNS ON THIS
LITTLE OVAL TRAY HARKS BACK TO THE
TREATMENT OF OUR PAINTED SCREEN. THE
DIFFERENCE IS ONE OF TRANSPARENT
DECORATION (MORE GUM ARABIC, LESS
GOUACHE COLOUR) AS MUCH AS OF A
LOOSER ARRANGEMENT.

CHAPTER EIGHT

Ribbons
& BOWS

The fashionable simplicity of fluttering ribbon streamers combines with the lighthearted prettiness of rococo bows. Cool Nordic colours and classic ornament create a fashionable Scandinavian look the Swedes call Gustavian after their most stylish King, Gustavus III. Keeping to a restrained colour scheme of greeny blues on cream, our Ribbons and Bows collection has an air of elegance.

The secret is not to overdo the ornament, but to use these motifs to underline the graceful proportions of a room or a piece of furniture. The result is serenely sophisticated in the best eighteenth-century Swedish manner, and would look as much at home in a city apartment as in a period country house.

COOL COLOURS CAPTURE THE

The only thing that the pieces of furniture in this room have in common is a certain purity of line which is especially suited to the understated style of the patterns in this book. Look for pieces of furniture with straight, slender legs and a minimum of fussy mouldings. Many Edwardian pieces of no

great value, in dark wood or veneer, have a latent quality which our restrained treatment brings out brilliantly. Notice how the Ribbons and Bows colour scheme is keyed into the equally calm decoration of the room itself. Again painted in blue and cream, the walls play off the pale blue beneath the dado rail

MOOD OF A MOMENT

against the broad stripes of blue and cream above. Use emulsion paint and masking tape to ensure the crisp, straight lines on which the elegant effect depends. The unified colour scheme and absence of fuss make for a spacious, classy effect which anyone could copy and feel comfortable with, for the Gustavian style is essentially unpretentious. A Swedish house of the period might well stand its painted furniture on bare boards of scrubbed pine, and restrict soft furnishings, as here, to a simple fall of muslin at the window and rustic checks for cushions and chair covers.

145

PAINTING WITH A PATTERN

With the help of our pull-out patterns and transfer paper, even absolute beginners can learn how to handle a range of motifs, from the simplest leaf-and-berry border to a fluttering rococo bow. Soon you will be able to create something as poised as the chair shown opposite.

Points to remember:
• Much of the delicacy and liveliness of the painted decoration shown here in close-up derives from the use throughout of artists' gouache dissolved in gum arabic, both materials obtainable from any artists' suppliers.
• Gouache is a vivid and concentrated form of watercolour in tubes, popular with illustrators and graphic designers because it is much easier to handle

than the classic type of watercolour pan (or block) sold in tin sets that everyone remembers from childhood.
• Gum arabic, a clear fluid, makes an excellent, controllable, transparent paint when tinted with gouache, adding fluency to brushwork and offering a wide range of tone - the more gouache you add to the gum arabic, the stronger and less transparent the colour.
• Only a few gouache colours were used to paint our motifs, the subtle tonalities being achieved simply by varying the dilution of gouache colours in gum arabic.
• Soft watercolour brushes, in sizes from medium to fine, are essential for a neat finish. But there is no need to buy expensive sable brushes - synthetic bristle or mixed hair are fine.

1 THE SIMPLE LEAF-AND-BERRY MOTIF, OFTEN SEEN AROUND THE RIM OF A VASE, IS FIRST TRACED DOWN WITH A SHARP PENCIL ABOVE A PIECE OF BLUE TRANSFER PAPER, CUT TO FIT FOR CONVENIENCE.

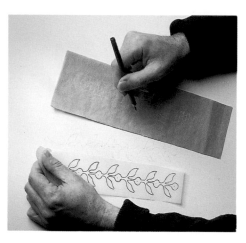

2 WITH THE TRANSFER PAPER LIFTED OFF, THE SIMPLICITY OF OUR TRACE-DOWN METHOD OF DECORATION IS CLEAR TO SEE.

3 USING A MEDIUM-FINE BRUSH DIPPED INTO COLOUR A, THE BASIC LEAF SHAPES ARE PAINTED IN. USE THE BRUSH TO CREATE DEPTH BY INCREASING PRESSURE AT THE FATTEST POINT OF THE LEAF. YOU MAY NEED TO PRACTISE THIS FIRST ON A PIECE OF PAPER.

5 USING COLOUR B (AND DILUTING THE GOUACHE COLOUR QUITE HEAVILY WITH GUM ARABIC) DARKER STROKES ARE ADDED TO THE UNDERSIDES OF THE LEAVES AND TO ONE SIDE OF THE BERRY SHAPES.

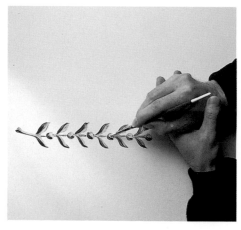

6 COLOUR C IS THEN APPLIED AS SHOWN TO CREATE HIGHLIGHTS ON THE OPPOSITE SIDE OF THE LEAF AND BERRY SHAPES.

7 RETURNING TO COLOUR B, THE DARK SHADING IS FILLED OUT AND EMPHASIZED FOR A SIMPLE THREE-DIMENSIONAL EFFECT. FINALLY, USE COLOUR C TO HIGHLIGHT THE DETAILS OF THE MOTIF.

NOTE: Transparent watercolour paint
is inherently more fragile than
emulsion and needs 'fixing' on
completion of decoration, *before* you
proceed to further varnishing,
antiquing etc. All the decoration in
this series was fixed with a rapid
blast of spray varnish, available from
artists' suppliers.

4 THE SAME BRUSH IS NEXT USED TO 'BLOB'
  IN THE ROUND BERRIES THAT ALTERNATE
WITH THE LEAVES, STRENGTHENING THE VISUAL
IMPACT OF THE STALK.

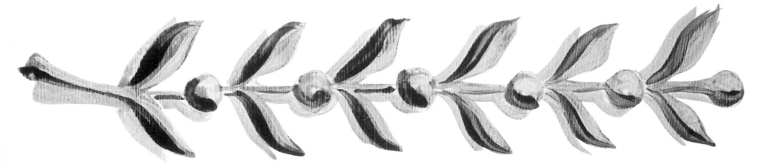

THE COMPLETED BORDER SHOWS HOW ARTFUL
BRUSHWORK AND A CONTROLLED USE OF
TONES, FROM LIGHT TO DARK, CAN MAKE A
VIVID LITTLE PASSAGE OF DECORATION FROM
THE SIMPLEST OF SHAPES.

COLOUR RECIPES
A ULTRAMARINE PLUS PERMANENT GREEN DEEP
B MORE ULTRAMARINE THAN A
C A PLUS FLAKE WHITE

The casual bow of ribbon with its fluttering ends and nonchalant grace is one of the timeless charmers of the ornamental repertoire. It is - or was - also notoriously testing to paint, but the step-by-step instructions for our trace-down bow make this versatile motif accessible to anyone who has mastered the techniques set out on the preceding pages.

1 THE BOW IS BUILT UP USING THE SAME TECHNIQUE OF SHADING FROM LIGHT TO DARK AS APPLIED FOR THE LEAF-AND-BERRY BORDER; BUT HERE THE BRUSHWORK IS MORE TENTATIVE, BEING COMPOSED OF SHORT STACCATO STROKES.

2 COLOUR B, THE DEEPEST TONE, IS SUPERIMPOSED OVER THE BASIC SHAPE (IN COLOUR A) USING THE FATTEST BRUSH IN A LOOSER MOVEMENT. IT SHOULD FEEL ALMOST AS IF YOU ARE LETTING THE BRUSH FIND ITS OWN WAY.

5 THE COMPLETED BOW DEFINES ITS FRAGILE DELICACY BY NOTHING MORE THAN THE CAREFUL GRADATIONS OF TONE AND AN OVERALL LIGHTNESS OF EXECUTION.

148

3 COLOUR C, THE LIGHTEST BLUE-GREEN TONE, HIGHLIGHTS SECTIONS OF RIBBON IN IMITATION OF LIGHT FALLING ON A REFLECTIVE FABRIC SUCH AS SATIN, SILK OR MOIRÉ.

4 THE SAME PALER TONE IS NOW USED TO 'FATTEN UP' SECTIONS OF THE BOW. THIS BACK-AND-FORTH STYLE IS NECESSARY BECAUSE EACH NEW STEP REQUIRES A NEW RESPONSE.

1 DIFFERENT SITUATIONS DEMAND DIFFERENT BOWS. THIS MORE PENDANT VERSION IS GOOD FOR CENTRING A BEDHEAD OR A PELMET, AND SERVES AS AN ANCHOR FOR ORNAMENT.

2 THE DEEPEST TONE, COLOUR B, GIVES DEPTH, EXPRESSION AND SHADING TO THE BASIC MID-TONE BOW SHAPE.

3 THE FINISHED BOW HAS TRAILING RIBBONS PAINTED IN COLOURS A AND B FOR A LIGHT BUT VIVID PRESENCE.

1 THE EXQUISITE PENDANT AND SWAG MOTIF IS COMPOSED OF REPEATED BELLFLOWERS. HERE THE BELLFLOWERS ARE BEING FILLED IN USING COLOUR A (AS USED FOR PREVIOUS PATTERNS).

2 THIS SHOWS THE COMPLETED MOTIF USING ONLY THE BASIC MID-TONE, COLOUR A. TRY TO KEEP THE PRESSURE THE SAME ON THE LEFT AND RIGHT SIDES OF THE MOTIF.

3 A DEEPER TONE, COLOUR B, IS USED TO INTENSIFY AND DRAMATIZE THE MOTIF BY SHADING AREAS AS SHOWN.

4 HIGHLIGHT THE SIDE OPPOSITE THE SHADED AREAS USING THE MID-TONE LIGHTENED WITH FLAKE WHITE (COLOUR C).

5 FINAL TOUCHES ARE ADDED, IN COLOURS B AND C, TO STRENGTHEN THE WHOLE MOTIF AND GIVE IT VIVACITY.

6 THE COMPLETED DESIGN HAS AN ELEGANCE AND LIGHTNESS OF TOUCH THAT EVEN ROBERT ADAM WOULD HAVE APPRECIATED.

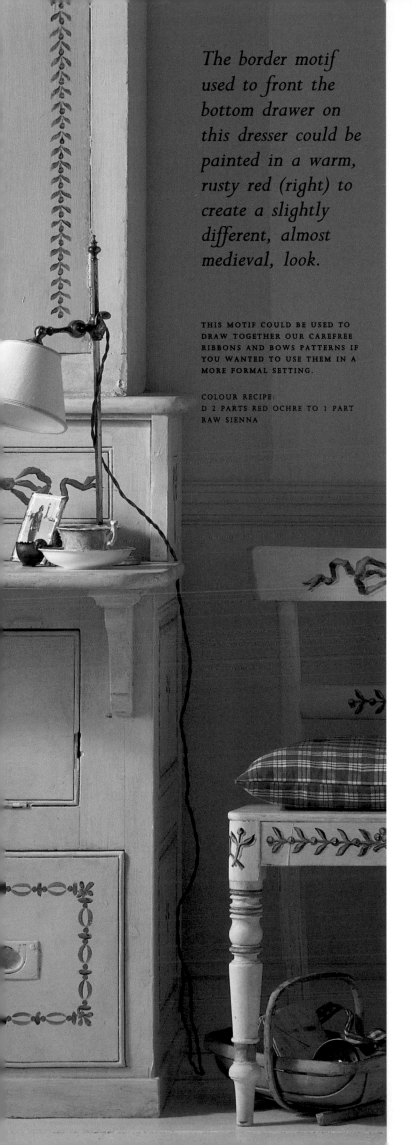

The border motif used to front the bottom drawer on this dresser could be painted in a warm, rusty red (right) to create a slightly different, almost medieval, look.

THIS MOTIF COULD BE USED TO DRAW TOGETHER OUR CAREFREE RIBBONS AND BOWS PATTERNS IF YOU WANTED TO USE THEM IN A MORE FORMAL SETTING.

COLOUR RECIPE:
D 2 PARTS RED OCHRE TO 1 PART RAW SIENNA

1 NOTICE HOW THE CORNER MOTIF FOR THIS BORDER PATTERN IS ACCURATELY ALIGNED WITH THE SECTION OF TRACED-DOWN BORDER SHOWN HERE FOR A NEAT EFFECT.

2 USE A MEDIUM BRUSH AND COLOUR D TO PAINT IN THE ROUNDED BARREL SHAPES USING THREE STROKES FOR EACH ONE. USE A BLOB OF PAINT FOR THE DOTS BETWEEN THE BARREL SHAPES.

3 WITH A SLIGHTLY DEEPER TONE OF THE SAME COLOUR (THAT IS, WITH A LITTLE MORE GOUACHE ADDED TO THE FORMULA) THE SHAPES ARE ENRICHED AND LIGHTLY SHADED FOR EMPHASIS.

DECORATIVE DETAILS CAPTURE THE CHARM

The right finish adds warmth and character to our suite of Ribbons and Bows.

Like the rest of the Ribbons and Bows furniture, this attractive bedside cupboard was base-painted in an ivory matt emulsion over acrylic primer. Afterwards, the watercolour decoration was applied and 'fixed' with spray varnish, and then the entire piece was given two final coats of protective varnish, each with a little colour added to lend a subtle warmth and age to the colour scheme and to make the ornament 'lie down' and blend harmoniously.

THIS CLOSE-UP DETAIL OF OUR BE-SWAGGED WINDOW SEAT SHOWS HOW THE INITIAL COLDNESS OF THE IVORY BASE HAS BEEN GIVEN A GOLDEN TINGE BY APPLYING A LIGHTLY TINTED VARNISH. USE A GOOD-QUALITY MATT VARNISH OR A MID-SHEEN POLYURETHANE FOR HEAVY-DUTY PROTECTION. REMEMBER THAT THESE ARE OIL-BASED, SO TINTING SHOULD BE DONE WITH A LITTLE ARTISTS' OIL TUBE COLOUR (RED OCHRE OR RAW SIENNA) DISSOLVED IN A LITTLE WHITE SPIRIT. STIR THIS INTO SOME DECANTED VARNISH, MIX WELL, AND THEN TEST IT FIRST ON AN INVISIBLE PATCH.

A whole package of bright ideas tied up with our Ribbons and Bows.

Once you have hit upon a winning theme like this one, it is an exciting challenge to think of new uses for the basic motifs. The beauty of traditional ornament is that it never looks dated or over the top. Designers have endlessly recombined these same pattern elements over the centuries, and the ideas shown here only hint at the range of possibilities.

WHEN IS A TRAY NOT A TRAY? WHEN THE ADDITION OF PAINTED CHEQUERS AND A LITTLE CUPBOARD BENEATH TURNS IT INTO A HANDY GAMES TABLE, WITH SPACE TO STORE THE PIECES AND OTHER PARAPHERNALIA. THE DISCREET PLACING OF OUR RIBBONS AND BOWS MOTIFS LIFTS A JUNK DUO INTO AN ELEGANT LITTLE PIECE THAT WOULD LOOK RIGHT AT HOME JUST ABOUT ANYWHERE.

THE PENDANT BOW PREVIOUSLY USED TO FILL IN A SMALL VERTICAL PANEL ON A BUREAU FINDS A NEW LEASE OF LIFE S-T-R-E-T-C-H-E-D AND PAINTED STRAIGHT ON TO THE WALL AS A VISUAL LINK FOR A FAVOURITE COLLECTION OF BLUE-AND-WHITE CHINA PLATES. THIS PRETTY IDEA LOOKS MORE EFFECTIVE WHEN PAINTED THAN IT WOULD WITH ANY REAL RIBBON.

STRIPED WALLS HAVE AN EIGHTEENTH-CENTURY FORMALITY, BUT ARE GIVEN A TWENTIETH-CENTURY LOOK HERE BY USING BROAD STRIPES OF MATT EMULSION PAINTED DIRECTLY ON TO THE PLASTER. USE A PLUMB LINE AND MASKING TAPE AS A GUIDE TO PAINTING THE STRIPES NEATLY.

THE LEAF-AND-BERRY BORDER IS ENOUGH TO LEND A CRISP NEW STYLE TO A VERY ORDINARY WOODEN TRAY. NOTE HOW THE MOTIF IS ARRANGED FOR SYMMETRY ON A LONG BORDER, WITH A CENTRAL BERRY AND THE BORDER GOING IN OPPOSITE DIRECTIONS EITHER SIDE. FOR GREATER DEFINITION, QUITE WIDE 'RULES' WERE ADDED ON THE BASE AND AROUND THE TOP, USING THE SAME TRANSPARENT WATERCOLOUR APPLIED FREE-HAND WITH A WATERCOLOUR BRUSH. ALTERNATIVELY, YOU MIGHT FIND THIS EASIER TO DO WITH A LONG BRISTLED LINING BRUSH, OR WITH MASKING TAPE TO DEFINE THE 'RULES'. BUT A FREE-HAND LINE WITH A SLIGHT WOBBLE ALWAYS LOOKS BETTER THAN ONE DONE WITH MASKING TAPE WHEN IT'S ON A SMALL SCALE SUCH AS HERE.

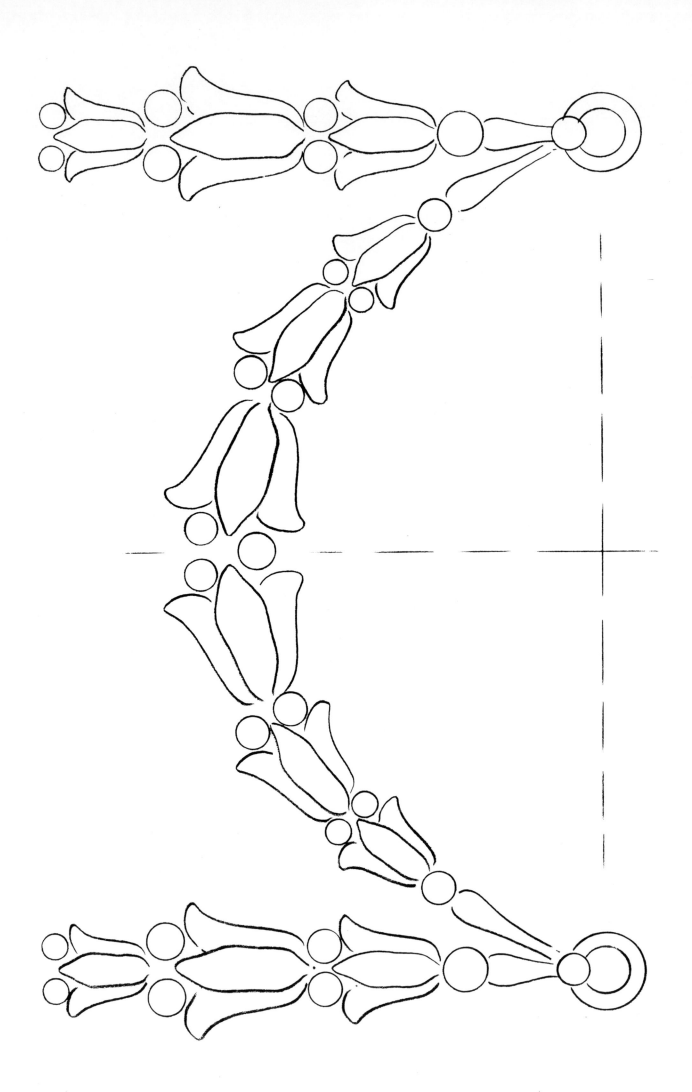

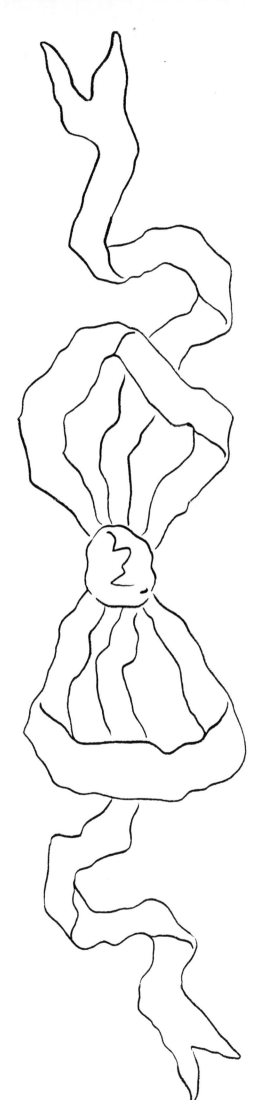

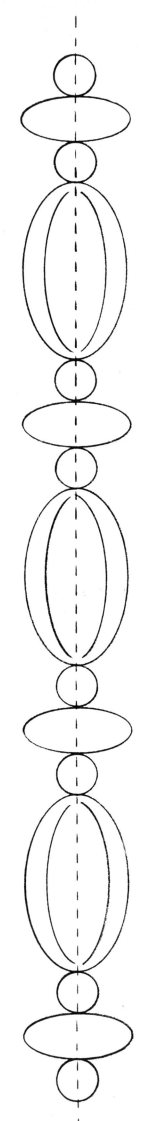